CRIME SCIENCE

CRIMINAL PROFILING

Matt Anniss

Gareth Stevens
Publishing

Please visit our website, www.garethstevens.com. For a free color catalog of all our high-quality books, call toll free 1-800-542-2595 or fax 1-877-542-2596.

Library of Congress Cataloging-in-Publication Data

Anniss, Matt.
Criminal profiling / by Matt Anniss.
  p. cm. — (Crime science)
Includes index.
ISBN 978-1-4339-9481-4 (pbk.)
ISBN 978-1-4339-9482-1 (6-pack)
ISBN 978-1-4339-9480-7 (library binding)
1. Criminal behavior, Prediction of — Juvenile literature. 2. Criminal profilers — Juvenile literature. 3. Criminal investigation — Juvenile literature. I. Anniss, Matt. II. Title.
HV8073.5 A56 2014
363.25—dc23

First Edition

Published in 2014 by
Gareth Stevens Publishing
111 East 14th Street, Suite 349
New York, NY 10003

© 2014 Gareth Stevens Publishing

Produced by Calcium, www.calciumcreative.co.uk
Designed by Keith Williams and Paul Myerscough
Edited by Sarah Eason and Jennifer Sanderson

Photo credits: Cover: Shutterstock: Margarita Borodina bl, Grafvision br, Ivan101 tc, Andrew Lever c, Georg Preissl t. Inside: Dreamstime: Annieannie 26, Chrisjo88 20, Eddiesimages 32, Fotosmurf02 1, 36, Jank1000 11, Jeffbanke 28, Martinmark 18, Miluxian 24, Rmwood 21, Rtimages 31, Showface 29, Starletdarlene 34, Trekandshoot 13; Shutterstock: Andrey Popov 10, Yuri Arcurs 40, Anthony Berenyi 38, Tyler Boyes 12, Kevin L Chesson 37, Corepics VOF 4, 17, Shawn Hempel 27, iQoncept 22, Denise Kappa 8, Mangostock 14, MaxyM 9, Mikeledray 45, Miker 15, Monkey Business Images 5, Nomad Soul 39, Rossco 23, Lisa S. 42, Simon G 43, Spirit of America 41, StockLite 25, Graham Taylor 16, Anatoly Tiplyashin 19, TX King 6, Wavebreakmedia 7, WilleeCole 44; United States Department of Justice 35b; Wikipedia: FBI Photos 33, German Federal Archives 30b, Dan Huse 35t.

Printed in the United States of America

CPSIA compliance information: Batch #CS13GS: For further information contact Gareth Stevens, New York, New York at 1-800-542-2595.

CRIME SCIENCE

CONTENTS

CRIME PROFILING

Tracking and catching criminals can be a difficult business. Although the police have many scientific methods of collecting and analyzing evidence, sometimes these are not enough to crack a case. This is why the science of crime profiling is so important.

New Science

Crime profiling is one of the newest methods in crime science. Crime profilers study where, when, and why crimes are committed. By doing this, crime profilers can learn a lot about who may have carried out a crime, and why it was committed. Some crime profilers are experts in the way criminals think, while others specialize in spotting patterns in where crimes take place. Some advise the police about how to reduce crime, while others are brought in to help catch dangerous criminals.

Some crime profilers work with crime-scene investigators to help them understand why a crime has been committed.

Study and Research

The various methods used by crime profilers are based on study and research, rather than traditional police work. Although many of the techniques have been tried, tested, and proven to work, others are based on what researchers call theories. A theory is an idea, backed up with a solid argument based on detailed study. Many scientific theories have changed the way we view the world, while others have later been proven to be incorrect. In the world of crime profiling, theories are constantly changing.

Crime profilers of the future all start out by attending universities. There, they study a science called criminology, which is the basis of all crime-profiling work. Universities play a huge role in crime profiling; it is the research carried out there that often forms the basis of crime-profiling methods.

Many would-be profilers attend college to learn the skills they need to help the police catch dangerous criminals.

CHAPTER ONE
CRIMINOLOGY

The basis of all crime profiling is criminology. This is the scientific study of crime. Many crime profiling techniques used by the police are based on criminology.

Criminology for Beginners

Criminology is not a new science. The term was first used by an Italian lawyer and university professor named Raffaele Garofalo in 1885. However, over the last 100 years, criminology has developed into a vast subject with many different ideas and theories.

Criminologists

People who study criminology are known as criminologists. It is their job to look at where and how frequently crimes take place, and why criminals break the law.

Some criminologists spend time talking to prisoners to try to find out why they turned to crime.

The Causes of Crime

Some criminologists look in detail at the things that influence criminal behavior, such as the world around us, where we live, and how much money we have. Others specialize in specific forms of crime. Criminologists study every aspect of crime in order to try to explain why it happens, and more importantly, how it can be stopped.

CRACKED

One of the oldest ideas in criminology is Rational Choice Theory. Does the individual make a conscious choice to commit crime? Supporters of this theory say that the way to deter people from choosing to commit crimes is to offer tougher punishments.

Contrasting Ideas

Because criminology is such a broad science, criminologists often disagree on the causes of crime. Over the years, many different theories have been put forward to explain criminal behavior. This is a natural part of science. New evidence may prove old theories to be incorrect, while scientists often disagree about what the evidence tells us. Theories are just ideas—it is how they are used in the fight against crime that is important.

Criminology can be a difficult subject to study because many of the theories contradict each other.

7

DIFFERENT THEORIES

Over the years, criminologists have put forward many different ideas to explain the causes of crime. Some are controversial, and others have been changed and adapted over time.

Choosing Crime

Criminologists have long argued over the causes of crime. The very first criminologists, known as the "Classical School of Criminology," believed that people choose to become criminals.

Some criminologists believe that having more police officers on the streets deters criminal behavior.

Developing Theories

Later, criminologists of the "Positivist School" argued that people turn to crime due to forces beyond their control, such as losing their job, knowing other criminals, or living in run-down areas. In the early twentieth century, "Chicago School" criminologists expanded on this idea. They believed that being poor and not doing well at school were two of the greatest causes of crime.

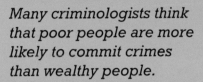

Many criminologists think that poor people are more likely to commit crimes than wealthy people.

Criminal Ideas

Since the early twentieth century, countless theories have been put forward to explain why people turn to crime. Some criminologists believe that certain people have a "criminal mind" and are therefore more likely to do terrible things. Other schools of thought believe that children inherit "criminal traits" from their parents.

Attitudes and Desire

Over time, attitudes toward certain crimes have changed, so people may not believe, or care, that they are breaking the law when committing these crimes. For instance, some criminologists argue that crime has increased because people are willing to break the law to get the latest must-have clothes and gadgets.

CRACKED

Criminologists have developed an idea called "Strain Theory." They argue that when money is tight, jobs are hard to come by, and people feel pressured by the strain of day-to-day life, they are more likely to turn to crime as a way out of their problems.

VICTIMOLOGY

One of the latest ideas in criminology theory is victimology. This is the study of victims of crime, how the crime affects them, and whether their actions put them at risk of attack.

Controversial Ideas

Some of the ideas put forward by victimologists are highly controversial. One theory is that some people are more likely to become victims of crime because of certain things they do. This could be doing a specific type of high-risk job, walking alone late at night, or being particularly friendly to strangers. This is a very unpopular idea because it suggests that victims of crime make themselves a target for criminals.

Victimologists often talk to victims of crime to find out how they have been affected.

Positive Steps

Victimology includes studying how people are affected by the crimes committed against them. By doing this, the police, courts of law, and governments can understand more about how people feel about crime, and what punishments should be given to criminals.

Victims' Rights

Today, more consideration is given to the rights of victims of crime. In the United States, victims are encouraged to go to court to explain how a crime has affected them. They are allowed to speak before the judge decides on the punishment of a convicted criminal.

BACK IN THE LAB

Some victimologists are employed by the government to study what effect crime has on victims, and how the legal system can make victims' lives more bearable. Others study crime data to try to figure out what sorts of people are more likely to be the victims of crime.

ENVIRONMENTAL CRIMINOLOGY

Many criminologists believe that the way people behave is influenced by their surroundings. They think that there is a direct link between where people live and whether they commit crimes.

Poverty Means Crime

There is a close link between crime levels—how many crimes happen—and poverty. More crimes happen in poor areas of cities. While some criminologists think that this is because there are fewer people with jobs and money is tight in these areas, environmental criminologists believe that the condition of buildings, the number of boarded-up properties, and how many parks and open spaces are present are just as important.

Trees Are Good

Some environmental criminologists think that the number of trees in an area has an effect on the crime rate. Research in Portland, Oregon, proved that levels of crime are significantly lower in areas where there are more large trees.

Environmental criminologists think that building wider streets, surrounded by trees, helps to reduce crime levels.

Building a Safer Community

Studies by environmental criminologists have also suggested that the height of backyard fences, the size and shape of windows, and the sort of street lighting used can also have an effect on crime rates. Because of this, town planners and architects have begun working with environmental criminologists when designing buildings and housing estates. They hope that by doing this, they will deter criminals from targeting these houses and the people who live there.

CRACKED

The idea of trying to reduce crime through the design of buildings and neighborhoods is called Crime Prevention Through Environmental Design (CPTED). Ideas regularly used by CPTED specialists include widening sidewalks to encourage more people to walk and bicycle around, adding trees to public areas, installing surveillance cameras, and making street lighting much brighter.

A neighborhood with plenty of trees and green spaces is less likely to be targeted by criminals than a built-up inner-city neighborhood.

15

CHAPTER TWO

CRIME ANALYSIS

Although criminology theories are the basis of all crime profiling, they do not always have a great deal of practical use for tackling crime. The same cannot be said of crime analysis, an area of criminal science that has revolutionized police work in the twenty-first century.

Practical Purpose

Crime analysis is examining all the available information about crimes in order to identify and predict trends. Police forces must record information about every crime reported, including where it was, who the victim was, and what sort of crime took place.

This information is stored on vast banks of computers and it is of great use to crime analysts. Not only can they use it to work out crime rates (the number of crimes that happen every week, month, or year), but they can also pinpoint exactly where crimes are taking place.

For crime analysis to be successful, police must report every tiny detail about a crime, including the location and "style" of crime.

POLICE LINE DO NOT CROSS

A greater police presence is often seen in areas where high-tech crime analysis of criminal activity has taken place.

Useful Information

Police forces all over the world use crime analysts to help them police the streets more effectively. If they know where, when, and what sort of crimes take place, then they can try to reduce crime. For example, if they know that there are more street crimes at night in a particular area, they can send out more police patrols at night to deter criminals. If the statistics show that drug users commit a lot of crimes, then they can put more resources into trying to catch drug dealers.

CRACKED

Crime analysts are often people who are really good at math. Every day, they have to trawl through software programs full of numbers and statistics to try to find trends. A trend is a pattern—for example, a rise in violent crime or a reduction in the number of teenagers committing crimes.

SOFTWARE AND STATISTICS

Crime analysis is a complicated process, but one that is changing the way the police tackle crimes. Using specially designed computer software, analysts can track the location, type, and frequency of crimes committed.

NYPD's Big Idea

The New York Police Department (NYPD) pioneered the use of crime analysis. In 1994, the NYPD started using a system called CompStat. CompStat used computer software to compile reports of all the crime committed in New York City.

CompStat

NYPD software allowed crime analysts to view maps of the city, which showed the location of the crimes. The system also included data on the police response, such as how many officers were sent to a crime scene. As part of the process, representatives from each of the city's 76 area precincts met to go through the crime-analysis information.

Special computer software allows police forces to track and log details of where crimes have happened.

Cutting Crime

CompStat is a huge success. According to NYPD officials, it has helped cut crime in the city dramatically. It also played an important role in cutting the number of murders from more than 1,100 in 1995 to 414 in 2012. Because of the system's success, it has since been adopted by police forces all over the United States, Canada, and the United Kingdom. By knowing all of the facts about where, when, and how often crimes happen, the police can more accurately manage their response to reported crimes.

CRACKED

Some police forces in the United States, Canada, and the United Kingdom have started allowing the public to see the location and details of crimes collected using the CompStat process. Using the website www.crimereports.com, you can get updates of where, when, and what sort of crimes are being reported.

SOLVING PROBLEMS

Crime analysis is now being used by police forces to identify the biggest crime problems in their area, so that they can tackle them head-on. This approach is called "problem-oriented policing."

Problem-Oriented Policing

Professor Herman Goldstein of the University of Wisconsin-Madison invented problem-oriented policing. Goldstein suggested to police forces that they combine crime analysis reports with the thoughts of police officers on the ground.

Treating the Root

In problem-oriented policing, officers are encouraged to use systems such as CompStat to spot crime trends (see pages 16–17). For example, by observing a rise in vandals breaking windows or convenience-store robberies, they may more easily find the cause of the crimes. By dealing with the root of the problem, the number of crimes of that type should drop dramatically.

Problem-oriented policing has been successfully used to cut down car crime in a number of US cities.

People Power

Most police forces that use problem-oriented policing try to involve the public. They actively encourage people to tell them about the problems in their area, often by holding weekly community meetings. In most areas where problem-oriented policing has been used, crime rates have dropped and confidence in the police has risen. When relations between the police and the public are at their best, crime is most likely to drop. After first being tested out in Wisconsin, problem-oriented policing has since been used in the United States in Maryland, New Jersey, North Carolina, and California, as well as in the United Kingdom.

By talking to the public about the crime problems in their area, police can gain vital information about criminal patterns in a particular place.

CHAPTER THREE

GEOGRAPHIC PROFILING

Geographic profiling is the "where" of modern policing. It uses advanced software to look at where crime is happening, either to identify patterns of criminal behavior or to help solve serious cases, such as serial killings or chains of robberies.

Where and Why

Geographic profiling is concerned with two things—where and why crimes take place. It is based on the old idea of crime mapping. In crime mapping, detectives would stick pins into a large map to see if there were any patterns between crime scenes and where evidence had been found.

Familiar Ground

Geographic profilers suggest that most criminals will commit their crimes in an area they know well. This could be close to where they live, an area in which they work, or somewhere they regularly go in their free time. Geographic profiling is most often used to help police with crimes that may be connected.

Geographic profiling has helped police to track down criminals, such as burglars and muggers who commit crimes in a small area.

Arson, a crime in which someone deliberately starts fires, is an area that has been targeted by geographic profilers.

Crime Patterns

Geographic profilers are specialists in spotting what they call "patterns of offender behavior." For example, if a serial killer was at large and all of the victims had been found close to bars, it would suggest that he or she picked them at random when out at night. In cases of serial crimes, such as murders or arson, more often than not there are patterns in the way criminals behave. These patterns are not always obvious, so geographic profiling can help find the criminal

CRIME MAPPING

The backbone of geographical profiling is crime mapping. Although now quite advanced, thanks to the use of computers, it has been used by police forces for many years for a number of reasons.

Pins in a Map

In the early days of crime mapping, police stuck pins into large maps. Originally, crime mapping was used in serious cases with multiple crimes to help narrow down the search for evidence. By looking at the location of the pins in the map, police could identify the best areas to look for clues.

Geographic Information Systems

In recent years, crime mapping has become much more sophisticated. Today's crime analysts use a type of computer software called Geographic Information Systems (GIS) to keep track of the location of crimes, spot trends, and advise police about crime hotspots.

Maps created using crime data help the police to find out which neighborhoods are the least safe. On this map of the United States, the areas shown in dark orange have the highest level of violent crimes.

Crime analysts who use crime mapping spend a lot of their time comparing many different types of information. In order to guide the police, they will compile presentations showing the exact location of specific crimes over a set period of time, the locations of certain types of crime, and how the police responded.

"Real time" crime-mapping information is used by police forces when deciding where to send officers.

Advanced Mapping

The GIS used by crime analysts allows them to look at many different types of information. They can, for example, compare the location of crimes with the locations of schools, betting establishments, bars, nightclubs, and housing areas. Doing this can help them understand the underlying causes of crime, and in turn suggest solutions to the problems. Crime mapping is a vital part of the CompStat system used by many police forces (see pages 16–17), and it has also been used to assist problem-oriented policing projects (see pages 18–19).

SOFTWARE SOLUTIONS

The days of sticking pins in maps mounted on the walls of police stations are long gone. Today, crime mapping and geographic profiling is carried out using advanced computer software programs.

Computer Assistance

Modern crime-mapping software is based on GIS (see page 22). These advanced computer programs combine mapping software with databases. A database is a program that allows users to store and search through huge amounts of information quickly and easily.

GIS Software

Using GIS software, crime analysts can search for information, which will then be displayed on a map or series of maps. The first-ever specialist geographic-profiling computer program was developed by Canada's Dr. Kim Rossmo. It was designed to help solve serial murder cases.

Today, old-fashioned paper maps have been replaced by high-tech computer systems to accurately mark where crimes have taken place.

The information stored in geographical-profiling and crime-mapping computer programs can be displayed as graphs and charts.

Leading Systems

There are now a number of specialist geographic-profiling software systems available to crime analysts. One of these is called Rigel Analyst. According to its makers, this program has a high success rate and can narrow down the likely home of a wanted criminal. They say it is 95 percent accurate. This means that it is correct in 95 out of 100 crimes. Another popular program used by many police forces is CrimeStat. This has features similar to Rigel Analyst, but can also help analysts figure out how far criminals travel to carry out their crimes.

BACK IN THE LAB

When hunting for serial killers, many police forces use a geographic-profiling progam called Gemini. Gemini has been designed specifically to figure out which crimes may belong to a series or are the work of the same criminal. It even ranks crimes in order of how likely they are to be part of a series.

25

THE CONS OF GEOGRAPHIC PROFILING

Although popular, geographic profiling is not always as successful as other profiling methods. According to critics of the theory, this is because it has serious limitations.

Limited Use

The biggest problem with geographic profiling is that it is concerned only with the locations of crimes. While some criminals may carry out their crimes in a certain area or in a pattern, this is not always the case. If detectives base their investigations on geographic-profile findings that turn out to be wrong, they will have wasted a lot of time and money. What is more, in that time, the criminal would be free to continue to carry out even more crimes.

Many Areas, One Criminal

Often geographic-profiling systems also overlook the fact that some criminals are prepared to travel large distances to carry out their crimes. If a serial killer murdered his or her victims in several areas or states, geographical profiling would be of little use.

Geographic profilers do not take into account the fact that some criminals commit crimes in several areas.

EXIT 7

9 AA HIGHWAY

Wilder
Maysville
3/4 M

Software Issues

The third worry that critics have is about the computer software itself. The results of geographic profiling will only ever be as good as the software being used and the information that is entered into the database. If the information is out of date, incorrect, or even misleading, the geographic profile will be inaccurate.

Use with Caution

Critics say that although geographic profiling can be a useful tool in serious crime cases, it should only ever be used with other methods, such as evidence gathering and interviewing witnesses.

REAL-LIFE CASE

Despite its limitations, geographic profiling does get results. In 2005, Raymond Lopez was arrested for robbing more than 200 houses in Orange County, California, after police used geographic-profiling software to predict where he lived. More police were sent to the area, leading to Lopez's arrest.

27

CHAPTER FOUR
OFFENDER PROFILING

The best-known area of crime profiling is offender profiling. Also known as psychological profiling, offender profiling has been featured in many movies and television series.

Who and Why

Offender profiling is the process of trying to figure out who committed a crime and why they did it, based on an understanding of criminal behavior. Offender profilers try to identify criminals by analyzing the crime, how it was committed, and any other relevant case evidence.

Studying the Clues

Criminals may leave clues at the crime scene about the type of person they are and how they think. Offender profilers also look in close detail at the choices criminals make before and after a crime, such as how well it was planned and the methods used to carry out the crime. These can also offer clues about the type of people they are.

Unlike geographic profiling, offender profiling is based on the careful examination of all case evidence.

SHERIFF'S LINE DO NOT CROSS

Criminal profilers examine case evidence carefully in order to find clues about the criminal's identity.

BACK IN THE LAB

Offender profilers divide their time between studying case evidence in order to create psychological profiles, teaching police detectives about basic profiling techniques, and learning more about how and why crimes are committed. They spend most of their time in an office and rarely visit crime scenes.

Human Behavior

Offender profilers often start out their career as psychologists. These are scientists who specialize in human behavior. They do not work on all cases and, in general, the police use them only to help catch very serious criminals. To help police, they must create a detailed description of the sort of person who may have committed the crime.

Patience and Knowledge

Offender profiling can be a tricky and time-consuming business, but if a criminal is caught, it is very rewarding. Offender profiling requires patience, an understanding of criminal behavior, and a knowledge of personality types (for example, whether someone is outgoing or introverted).

THE HISTORY OF OFFENDER PROFILING

The psychological profiling of criminals is not a new development. It has been used in different forms since the nineteenth century. Over the years, a number of famous profilers have helped develop the science behind the technique.

Jack the Ripper

The first offender profiler was a British doctor named Thomas Bond. During the 1880s, he studied the crimes of a famous murderer nicknamed "Jack the Ripper." After looking in detail at the Ripper's crimes, he worked out that the killer was likely to be a quiet, middle-aged man who was "strong, composed, and daring."

Predicting Hitler

During World War II, the US government asked psychologist Dr. Walter C. Langer to create an offender profile of the Nazi leader, Adolf Hitler. To create his profile, Langer studied Hitler's books and listened to recordings of his speeches. Langer predicted that Hitler would kill himself if he lost the war. That is exactly what happened in April 1945.

Dr. Walter C. Langer's psychological profile of Adolf Hitler was crucial in helping the Allies to win World War II.

Bomb Squad

In the 1950s, a psychologist named James A. Brussel helped police to track down a terrorist who had planted bombs in New York City over a 16-year period. Brussel studied the case files and figured out that the bomber was likely to be a "heavy" middle-aged mechanic who once worked for the Consolidated Edison power company. The description helped the police to catch George Metesky, whose appearance and background accurately matched Brussel's profile. The case inspired the FBI to take the technique more seriously.

FBI psychological profilers work closely with detectives while investigating murder cases.

REAL-LIFE CASE

Offender profiling helped the FBI to track down one of the United States' most dangerous serial killers, Ted Bundy. Offender profiling specialist Dr. Richard B. Jarvis provided police with a description that accurately predicted Bundy's age, characteristics, and above-average intelligence.

THE FBI METHOD

In the United States, offender profiling is carried out using a special five-phase technique called the FBI profiling method. This was developed by two of the fathers of modern offender profiling, John E. Douglas and Robert Ressler.

Stage One

The FBI profiling method uses five different stages to create an accurate profile of a dangerous criminal, usually a murderer. First, profilers examine all available case information and evidence, from crime-scene photos and victim profiles to police reports and witness statements. This is known as the "assimilation stage."

Stage Two

The second stage is called the "classification stage." In this stage, profilers decide whether the criminal is organized or disorganized. Organized criminals often plan their crimes in detail, while disorganized criminals usually do not plan attacks and often leave lots of evidence.

During the "assimilation stage," profilers carefully study all case evidence from a crime scene in detail.

Students at the FBI Academy are taught the techniques behind the world-famous FBI profiling method.

Before and After

In the third stage, profilers focus on the criminal's behavior before and after the crime. The idea is to try to figure out the exact sequence of events in order to learn not only how the crime was committed, but also what it says about the criminal's personality. When that is complete, the profilers look for the criminal's "signature." This is anything the criminal does at the scene of the crime that is different or unusual and may give a clue about the way he or she thinks. The final stage of the FBI method is to create a profile for detectives to use.

CRACKED

John E. Douglas is one of the most successful FBI criminal psychologists of all time. During the 1970s, he worked at the FBI's Behavioral Sciences Unit, where he taught his famous FBI method of profiling. He retired in 1995, but is still asked by police forces to help in the hunt for serial killers.

33

THE BEHAVIOR ANALYSIS UNIT

The FBI has a special department dedicated to psychological analysis and offender profiling. It is part of the National Center for the Analysis of Violent Crime (NCAVC), and it is called the Behavior Analysis Unit (BAU).

BAU

The BAU came into being in the 1970s, after the successful launch of Robert Ressler's Behavioral Sciences Unit. The Unit is based in Virginia and takes responsibility for most offender profiling undertaken by the FBI.

Profilers from the BAU are regularly asked by detectives investigating serious cases to go to crime scenes.

Handy Help

When police forces and FBI departments are hunting killers or other dangerous criminals, they often contact the BAU for help. Sometimes, the BAU sends profilers around the country to help investigators. At other times they offer advice over the telephone. They also offer training for FBI agents in the basic principles of offender profiling.

Television shows such as Criminal Minds are watched by millions of viewers. Actor Thomas Gibson plays Aaron Hotchner, the Unit Chief of the BAU.

Investigative Analysis

The BAU specializes in "criminal investigative analysis." Criminal investigative analysis involves looking closely at serious crime, criminal behavior, and also the investigation itself to help detectives crack difficult cases. The Unit carries out its tasks using a number of different methods, from offender profiling and traditional crime analysis to advising detectives on how best to manage manhunts for serial killers.

BACK IN THE LAB

One of the ways in which BAU profilers use their knowledge of criminal behavior is to advise detectives on what to ask suspected criminals during police interviews. They devise a series of questions that are most likely to result in a confession from the criminal.

Specialist Staff

Most of the Unit's staff members are experienced criminal profilers specializing in violent crimes such as murder, crimes against children, or terrorism. The Unit's scientific approach and great knowledge of criminal behavior has helped bring many dangerous criminals to justice over the last 20 years.

LINKAGE ANALYSIS

One of the tasks often performed by BAU crime profilers is linkage analysis. This technique brings together elements of criminal and geographic profiling to figure out if a series of crimes is linked.

Connected Events

Linkage analysis is a method used by profilers and police detectives to figure out whether a series of crimes was committed by the same criminal. For example, police could be investigating a series of killings in different states that was carried out over a long period of time. They may not look like they are connected, but by carrying out detailed linkage analysis, criminal profilers may be able to prove that they were the work of the same criminal. When carrying out linkage analysis, criminal profilers will try to use their understanding of criminal behavior to spot patterns that link the crimes together.

Crime-scene evidence that looks out of place could link a crime to others that have previously happened in other areas of the country.

The tiniest piece of evidence could provide a link between the crime being investigated and the criminal.

CRACKED

Police in Canada use a special software system to carry out linkage analysis. Called the Violent Crime Linkage Analysis System (ViCLAS), it has so far helped prove links between serial criminals and more than 80,000 crimes.

Clues in Maps

Today, linkage analysts will often carry out geographic profiling as part of the process. This is to see whether there are additional links or clues in the location of the crimes or where bodies were discovered in murder cases.

Last Hope

Generally, linkage analysis is a last resort for detectives working on murder cases. It is used only in rare cases where evidence is limited. Often, crimes are solved using DNA evidence, which can provide clues about a criminal's identity, or fingerprint marks left at the crime scene. When this type of evidence does not exist, detectives may turn to linkage analysis.

PROBLEMS WITH PROFILING

Although offender profiling is hugely popular with the public and is often used by the police, critics say it is not very reliable. They say it is not nearly scientific enough, and when profiles prove to be incorrect, it can waste valuable police time.

Mistakes

The biggest problems with offender profiling happen when profilers make mistakes. If they assess all the evidence and tell police to look for a particular type of person, more often than not, detectives will put great faith in their opinion. If the profile turns out to be incorrect, the police will be searching for the wrong person and may even arrest someone who is totally blameless. This happened in 1996, when security guard Richard Jewell was arrested for bombing Centennial Park in Atlanta during the Olympic Games. Jewell's arrest gave the real bomber, Eric Rudolph, time to carry out two more bomb attacks.

The incorrect arrest of Richard Jewell for the Centennial Park bombings in Atlanta proved that offender profiling does not always work.

> *Critics of offender profiling say that it can lead to innocent people being arrested for crimes they did not commit.*

Not Enough Science

Critics of offender profiling say that it is impossible to draw conclusions about somebody's personality, background, and appearance from what they do when committing a crime. They argue that detectives should not read too much into the way someone behaves before and after they have committed a crime, because they may be acting differently due to the pressure of the situation.

REAL-LIFE CASE

The hunt for serial killer Gary Ridgway, better known as the "Green River Killer," was hampered by a partly incorrect profile. The offender profile drawn up by the FBI said that the killer was an outdoorsman and could not get close to other people. In fact, Ridgway was not an outdoorsman and had been married. The profile was wrong.

CHAPTER FIVE

INTO THE FUTURE

As a new science, crime profiling is by no means perfect. However, every year it is growing in popularity, with new ideas being put forward and techniques being developed.

Problems to Solve

All of the methods, techniques, ideas, and theories of offender profiling have good and bad points. Criminologists and crime profilers understand this and are working hard to increase their understanding of criminals, their behavior, and the science of catching them.

By comparing crime trends and statistics from different parts of the world, criminologists hope that they can learn more about the causes of crime.

Compare and Contrast

One of the latest developments in criminology is the idea of comparative criminology. This is the study of crime across different countries and groups of people (for example, those who earn a certain amount of money or follow a certain religion). The idea is to try to identify differences and similarities between crime rates and types of crime. By doing this, criminologists may be able to figure out the major causes of crime and how they could be tackled in the future.

Leading criminologists believe the best way to cut crime would be to improve the lives of those living in poor areas.

Crime Prevention

One idea that has gained popularity in recent years is crime prevention as a way of lowering crime rates. The idea is to stop, or prevent, people from turning to crime in the first place. Many criminologists have spent years studying which approaches work.

Tackling Poverty

In 2004, some of the world's leading criminologists put together a report listing the best ways to prevent crime. They suggested that countries should work together to tackle the global drug trade and focus more on the problems that cause crime, such as poverty.

BACK IN THE LAB

Some of the busiest crime profilers are forensic psychiatrists. These are scientists with a deep knowledge of how the human mind works. They are often used in court cases to pass judgment on whether or not criminals have any mental illnesses that may make them act differently.

INVESTIGATIVE PSYCHOLOGY

New, cutting-edge scientific techniques are being developed all the time to help crime profilers do their job. One of the latest is investigative psychology.

Research Is Key

Investigative psychologists, so-called because they investigate with methods that are similar to those used by detectives, are not unlike offender profilers. However, they take a much more scientific approach. Investigative psychologists try to help police by basing their conclusions on scientific research, rather than their own experiences of criminal behavior.

Different Approach

Investigative psychology differs from the FBI method of profiling, which asks criminal profilers to "think like the criminal." Investigative psychologists may assist the police with their work but spend most of their time carrying out research and studying case evidence and human behavior.

Investigative psychologists study all aspects of human behavior in order to figure out why people commit crimes such as burglary.

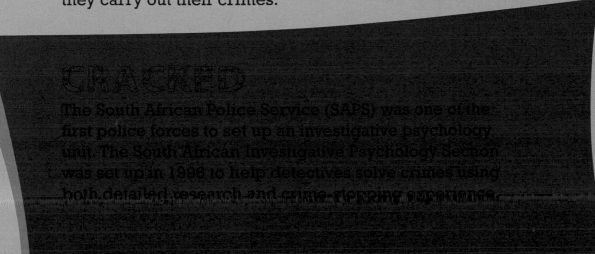

Investigative psychology has helped many countries solve homicides.

Finding Patterns

Some of the techniques used by investigative psychologists are similar to those used by crime analysts. They are just as interested in numbers as they are in the way people think. They want to try to prove links between patterns of behavior found in violent criminals, such as being aggressive, and how they carry out their crimes.

The Importance of Research

Investigative psychologists think that by carrying out detailed research, they will create much more accurate offender profiles in the future. Leading investigative psychologists believe that in the future they will understand far more about criminal behavior than regular crime profilers.

CRACKED

The South African Police Service (SAPS) was one of the first police forces to set up an investigative psychology unit. The South African Investigative Psychology Section was set up in 1996 to help detectives solve crimes using both detailed research and crime-fighting experience.

YOUNG SCIENCE

In the last 30 years, crime profiling has gone from an experimental technique to one of the cornerstones of modern policing. It has revolutionized the way crimes are investigated.

Modern Science

Crime mapping helps police forces to cut down crime and better plan their response to urgent calls from the public. Geographic profiling has helped detectives to pinpoint the whereabouts of many violent criminals, murderers, and arsonists.

Thanks to psychological offender profiling, detectives now better understand the way criminals behave and how they may think. Crime analysis allows police to quickly spot crime trends, while problem-oriented policing has improved many lives by cutting crime.

Although it is a young science, criminal profiling has helped to catch and convict dangerous criminals.

Shaping the Future

Many policing advances would not have happened without modern crime-profile techniques. Crime rates in many major US cities, such as New York City and Los Angeles, have been falling for many years, thanks in part to these techniques.

New Science

Crime profiling is not without fault. We need to remember that it is a new science. All of its methods are constantly being looked at, altered, and improved. Research by criminologists and psychologists will help shape the future of all detective work. Policing mistakes may still be made, but far more criminals will be caught.

REAL-LIFE CASE

Dr. David Canter is one of the most successful crime profilers of all time. In 1986, he created Britain's first-ever crime profile, which helped police catch a dangerous criminal known as the "Railway Killer." Canter gave 17 descriptions of the wanted man and 13 of them turned out to be correct.

GLOSSARY

adapted changed

analysis a detailed study of something

architect somebody who designs buildings for a living

arson deliberately setting fire to things

attitude how someone thinks about something

committed carried out a crime

controversial something that is unpopular or goes against popular thinking

convicted criminal somebody who has been judged guilty of a crime by a court of law

crime rates also called crime levels, these are statistics used by the police to show whether the number of crimes in a town or city have gone up or down

criminology the scientific study of crime

data information

database a computer software program for storing and sorting information

deter to put off

evidence something that proves an idea right or wrong, or (in criminal cases) that proves that somebody is guilty of something

experts people who know a lot about a certain subject

FBI short for the Federal Bureau of Investigation, a government agency belonging to the United States Department of Justice

manhunt an extensive search for a criminal

offender a criminal

research looking into something in great detail in order to learn more about it

resources any money, people, or equipment that can be used by an organization (for example, the police)

revolutionized dramatically changed

serial a series of connected crimes (for example, robberies, or a sequence of events)

serial killer someone who has killed a number of people

software program something on a computer designed to do a particular task, such as send e-mail, look at the Internet, or play games

statistics facts based on numbers, usually arrived at after collecting information or carrying out research. Crime rates are usually presented as statistics.

surveillance watching, looking, or listening, using cameras and other recording equipment

theory an idea backed up by evidence, usually based on research

vandals criminals who damage things on purpose (for example, windows, houses, or cars)

victim someone who has a crime committed against them (for example, somebody who has been attacked or robbed)

FOR MORE INFORMATION

BOOKS

Brown, Jeremy. *Crime Files: Four-Minute Forensic Mysteries.*
New York, NY: Scholastic, 2006.

Beres, D. B., and Anna Prokos. *Crime Scene: Profilers and Poison.*
New York, NY: Scholastic, 2009.

King, Colin. *Detective's Handbook.* London, UK: Usborne, 2008.

Levy, Janey. *Careers in Criminal Profiling.* New York, NY:
Rosen Central, 2009.

WEBSITES

Find out what a criminal profiler does and how you could take up a career in criminology at:
**www.criminologycareers.about.com/od/Career_Profiles/a/
Criminal-Profiler.htm**

Read more about crime mapping and its usefulness to the police at:
www.gislounge.com/crime-mapping-gis-goes-mainstream/

Find out what happens at a crime scene investigation and how specialists such as crime profilers assist investigations at:
www.howstuffworks.com/csi.htm

INDEX

UNION
Steamship Co.
OF BRITISH COLUMBIA, LIMITED
ESTABLISHED 1889

The Path of Sunshine and Sea Charm
along the
GULF COAST RIVIERA
by
UNION STEAMSHIPS
A Wonderland of Mountain and Marine Scenery

THE SUNSHINE COAST

THE SUNSHINE COAST

FROM GIBSONS TO POWELL RIVER
REVISED SECOND EDITION

HOWARD WHITE
PHOTOGRAPHY BY DEAN VAN'T SCHIP
KEITH THIRKELL, ALLAN FOREST, DARREN ROBINSON
AND OTHERS

HARBOUR PUBLISHING

CONTENTS

Pages 2–3: View from Soames Hill, Gibsons.

This spread: Granthams Landing.

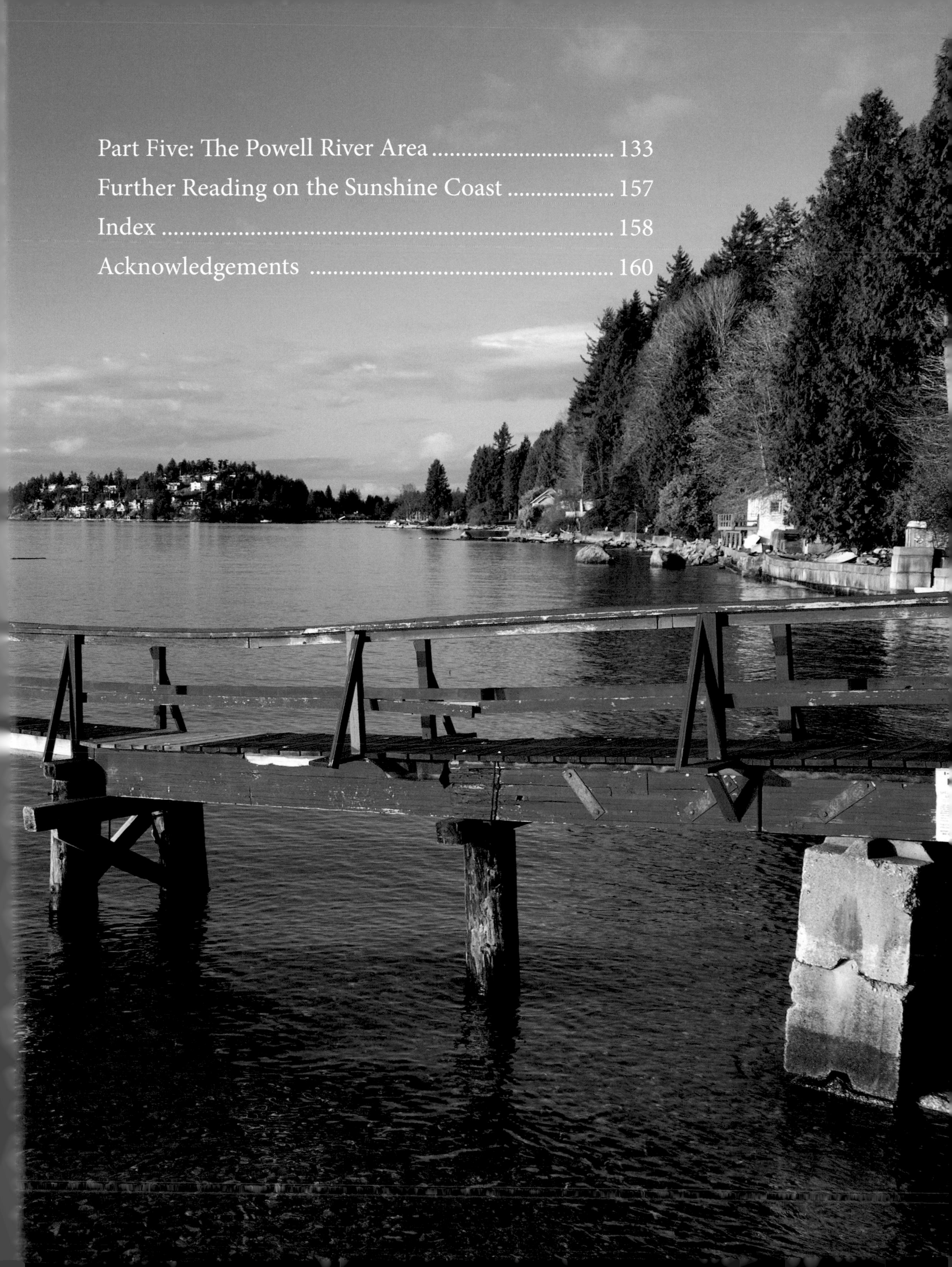

INTRODUCTION
THE SUNSHINE COAST

UNTIL THE 1980s, the sublimely scenic 100-mile stretch of shoreline along the eastern side of Georgia Strait known as the Sunshine Coast enjoyed a blessed obscurity that allowed its forty-thousand-odd residents to indulge their oddness to the fullest. The area has a reputation for being the maverick among British Columbia's favoured south coast regions and seems to rejoice in it. In the past fifteen provincial elections, the Sunshine Coast has voted against the government of the day eleven times, a contrariness that has rewarded the area with some of the twistiest sections of Highway 101 north of Guatemala.

The oddball image works for geography as well as politics. It's not an island, but you have to take a ferry to get there—five different ferries if you want to see all of it. Local developers have spent years dreaming of bridges, tunnels, overland links and fast commuter ferries aimed

The Sunshine Coast Highway is both sublimely scenic and seriously twisty.

Previous pages: The scenic ferry crossing from Saltery Bay to Earls Cove links the upper and lower Sunshine Coast.

at breaching the isolation of the Sunshine Coast while the old-time residents scheme just as determinedly to preserve it. The split between those who wish to conjoin with the growth convulsing BC's Lower Mainland just across the water and those who want to preserve the coast's quiet backwater status provides the spark that animates local politics. At one point in the early 1990s the area was served by no fewer than nine regularly published newspapers, and still there was never enough room to carry all the letters to the editor that flare up around such issues as improving the Westview–Comox ferry service or allowing the first McDonald's restaurant onto the Sechelt Peninsula.

Being neither fish nor fowl from a geographic standpoint, the Sunshine Coast lacks some of that romantic aura that attracted urban hordes to the true islands of the Gulf, leaving the area to evolve in its own way. Among those in the know it has long been seen as a haven where people might do their own thing in their own time with a minimum of interference from the outside world. This has made it a refuge for painters, writers, hermits, handloggers, stump ranchers, trappers, prospectors, fishermen, and draft dodgers of every war since the original of the Egmont Jeffries jumped ship during the 1859 Pig Wars in the San Juan Islands. They and other fugitives from the twentieth century established a string of quiet little villages whose names, from Hopkins Landing to Secret Cove to Gillies Bay, reflect their salty sense of self-possession.

It took until the mid-1980s for the area's attractions to be discovered in a major way, and by the early 1990s the Sunshine Coast was the fourth fastest-growing residential area in BC, to the chagrin of many of those longtime seekers of peace and quiet. But it remains one of the few places within commuting distance of Vancouver where you can still experience some of the sights and scents of the old-time BC coast of the steamships and the stump ranches, the

float camps and the fish plants. Villages like Lund and Pender Harbour still cling to their rocky shorelines like a fringe of storm-tossed driftwood, connected by red-railed boardwalks; Gambier and Savary Island children still ride to school in sea-going schoolbuses; and tide-borne seaweed, shovelled into gunny bags and wheeled up the beach trail in the wheelbarrow, is still the fertilizer of choice for home vegetable gardens throughout the region.

PARTS OF THE SUNSHINE COAST have enjoyed their own separate renown for decades.

The city of Powell River at the northern end of the territory, still the largest single community in the region, has been a destination for ocean-going ships since the world's largest pulp and paper mill was built there on the world's shortest river in 1910.

Nearby Desolation Sound has been known to discriminating boaters as one of the Pacific Northwest's most enchanting cruising experiences since Capi Blanchet immortalized it in her 1950s yachting classic, *The Curve of Time*. The feature attraction is an enchanted maze of islands and lagoons called Prideaux Haven, which by the 1980s had become the most popular marine park in the province.

Jervis Inlet, a mountain-girt fifty-mile-long fjord that cleaves the Sunshine Coast into north and south sections of roughly equal mass and population, has been a must-see for travellers of the world for generations. Princess Louisa Inlet, a canyon-like offshoot near the head of Jervis, attracted the likes of John Barrymore and Andrew Carnegie, who paid homage to its fabled mile-high splendour back in the early years of the twentieth century.

View looking up Malaspina Strait toward Powell River.
Darren Robinson

Right: Desolation Sound is the most popular boating area on the West Coast.

Below: Prideaux Haven, a maze of small islands and interlocking lagoons, is the jewel of Desolation Sound.

Just to the south, Skookumchuck Rapids at the entrance to Sechelt Inlet has graduated into legend as one of North America's most awesome saltwater cataracts, the sea-going graveyard of dozens of unwary small boaters. Both scenic wonders have thankfully been preserved as parks, though not before the north side of the Skookumchuck was transformed into a giant open-pit gravel mine. Timber companies continue to gnaw at the forest around Princess Louisa, rather in the spirit of old-time Athens businessmen grinding up the Parthenon to make cement (Gotta keep the boys busy).

Pender Harbour, an eccentric fishing community built around a jigsaw puzzle of coves, reefs and sloughs, where some people still do their Saturday shopping in small motorized "kicker" boats, has long been known as "The Venice of the North," and once served as the bustling winter capital of the populous shíshálh First Nation.

Anchoring the southern end of the Sunshine Coast, the town of Gibsons (I still like to call it Gibsons Landing, though it deep-sixed the "Landing" in 1947) boasts perhaps the West Coast's most familiar sea front. It was imprinted on millions of minds all over the globe during its nineteen years as the setting of the popular CBC television drama *The Beachcombers*.

BEGINNINGS

YOU MIGHT THINK THE SCENIC ATTRACTIONS alone would have sparked a more general interest in the Sunshine Coast, but a full century elapsed between the beginnings of European settlement in the late nineteenth century and the boom of the 1990s.

Non-First Nations history on the Sunshine Coast began with the arrival of the Spanish explorer José Maria Narváez in 1791 followed in 1792 by an English expedition under Captain George Vancouver. Both churned through the territory in such a panic to find the fabled Northwest Passage they failed to notice Sechelt Inlet, Pender Harbour and a host of other major geographical features. They did find time, however, to replace the poetic and myth-laden Native names which had served to identify the area's islands and inlets for thousands of years with the names of minor naval officials, school chums, mistresses, etc. The names for Thormanby Islands, Merry Island, Buccaneer Bay, Epsom Point, and Derby Point were inspired by an English horse race.

In other areas, southern Vancouver Island for instance, Native names were widely adopted by the new settlers and today give a special flavour to the area—Saanich, Malahat, Cowichan, Nanaimo. Sharkain, Chichatomos, Tsawcome—names that reflected the Sechelt's long and intimate relationship with the geography of the Sunshine Coast are all but lost. Apart from some less prominent geographical sites such as Sakinaw Lake near Pender Harbour and Clowhom Lakes up Salmon Inlet, the only major Sechelt name to survive is Sechelt itself, although "Sechelt" was not originally a place name, but rather the name of the shíshálh people themselves.

Over the years more explorers came to fill in the blanks left in the charts by Vancouver and Narváez—George Richards in 1860 and Daniel Pender in 1863, but no settlers followed in their wakes until the late 1880s. By then, the arrival of the trans-continental railway in Vancouver, and the Pre-Emption Act of 1884, which made it easier to obtain Crown land, had shifted BC development into high gear. Sechelt was the site of one of the first attempts by a European to take up land for settlement on the Sunshine Coast when John Scales, a decommissioned Royal Engineer fresh from building the Cariboo wagon road, was awarded a 260-acre homestead there in 1869. But the preemption lay unoccupied until it was purchased by Sechelt's first real non-First Nations settler, Thomas John Cook. Cook and his family didn't get

The Thormanby Islands are the site of one of the coast's largest marine parks and contain some of its finest beaches.

Previous spread: The public dock at Gibsons is the site of one of the coast's busiest small boat harbours.

established until 1890, about the time other settlers were staking out waterfront preemptions all along the Sunshine Coast from Port Mellon to Prideaux Haven.

Up on Texada Island things began stirring a little earlier when the BC premier of the day, Amor de Cosmos (a.k.a. Bill Smith), jointly purchased 50,000 acres for development as an iron mine in 1874. De Cosmos was forced to resign in the ensuing scandal, but eventually the iron mine did get up and running, providing the Sunshine Coast with its first two towns. The twin cities of Van Anda and Texada City boasted "three hotels and saloons, a hospital, a variety of stores and businesses, a local newspaper (*The Coast Miner*), a jail, and an opera house." The mine fizzled out in 1916, but other mines and businesses intent on exploiting Texada's immense limestone and mineral deposits kept the community alive.

CHRONICLES OF EUROPEAN SETTLEMENT ON the lower Sunshine Coast usually begin with the story of George Gibson, a gangling British naval officer who took out the first preemption in what would become Gibsons Landing in 1886, but I have never found old George had much to recommend him except the fact he somehow managed to wash up on these shores before most anybody else of the non-Native persuasion. Dour and stolid, he always struck me as an unfortunate person to erect a founding myth upon.

Texada Island has been a mining centre since the 1800s.

My candidate for Founding Spirit of the Sunshine Coast is Harry Roberts, the patron saint of Roberts Creek, who didn't arrive until 1900 but was much more the classic Sunshine Coast personality than Gibson. Imaginative, visionary, non-conforming to a fault—he literally put

Far left: The hard life of the pioneer shows in the faces of George and Charlotte Gibsons, founders of Gibsons Landing. Their dog, on the other hand, seems to have the best of all possible worlds. *Sunshine Coast Museum & Archive, 1726*

Left: Businessman, artist, philosopher—Harry Roberts was a pioneer of many parts. *Sunshine Coast Museum & Archive, 1050*

Below: Harry Roberts retreated to his pioneer homestead, "Sunray," on Nelson Island after making Roberts Creek too popular.

the Sunshine Coast on the map. An art student in England and later a painter, author and homespun philosopher, Roberts was the first Sunshine Coast pioneer to put into practice the idea that there are other things to do here just as important as cutting the trees, catching the fish, and doing the developments. But he also forged a bit of an industrial empire around Roberts Creek between the turn of the century and 1930. He even built himself a castle, albeit a wooden one. Then he chucked it and took to sea in his trusty yawl the *Chack-Chack* where he could paint, write and philosophize full-time, eventually resettling on a paradisical south-facing beach at Cape Cockburn on Nelson Island. There he constructed his celebrated second home, "Sunray," raised his three children, and kept house with his second and third wives, give or take.

Sunshine Coast pioneer Jim Spilsbury tells a story about Harry during his Sunray days that provides a glimpse of his uncommon character. For years Spilsbury and his wife, Win, summered on a choice piece of waterfront on Ballet Bay near Cape Cockburn which they had purchased from a crusty Norwegian boatbuilder named Sandvold. Sandvold was a bachelor, but not quite a confirmed one, it would seem. During the time in question, Harry Roberts felt called upon to take long absences from his wife, Cherry, in order to beachcomb, trade, paint, philosophize, philander—Harry himself never knew quite what he was up to at any given moment. Cherry had apparently quit caring and had taken to relieving her loneliness by entertaining Sandvold. Something tipped Harry off, so he pretended to leave on a trip but anchored in Quarry Bay and doubled back through the bush in time to catch Sandvold docking his fishboat at the Roberts dock in Cockburn Bay. Confirming his worst suspicions by peeping through the bedroom window, Harry considered his situation. He was wiry enough, but a flyweight. He weighed maybe 140 pounds soaking wet, while his rival was in the 200 range. Irate as he was, our Harry was no fool. He retreated quietly up the path and made his way over the hill to the dock, where he stepped aboard Sandvold's boat—and climbed up the rigging. When the big Norwegian came tromping down the gangplank in the wee hours of the morning, whistling and looking quite pleased with himself, Harry took a flying leap and landed on his adversary's head. Before Sandvold knew what hit him, Harry was all over him, thrashing him senseless with a cod bonker and cutting his boat adrift on the tide. Sandvold eventually recovered and had the bad grace to charge Harry with assault. When they appeared before the redoubtable magistrate William "Judge" Parkin in Powell River, Parkin listened as Sandvold began relating his complaint, frowned, then interrupted.

"Do you mean to stand there and tell me a strapping great oaf like *you* needs this court's help to protect you from a puny little runt like *him*?"

"He yoomp! He yoomp from de sky, your highness..."

"Case dismissed!"

HARRY WAS TYPICAL OF THE SLIGHTLY OFF-centre types who sifted over the hills and fetched up like continental driftwood here at the ocean's edge because they were too haywire to fit in more organized portions of the globe, but that is not the only reason I nominate him as the area's chief historical mascot. It was Harry's fertile brain that hatched the idea of combining all the coast's isolated settlements and landmarks under one regional name-tag so that in future, TV weathermen would have something to call the part of the province that remained after they'd listed off the Yukon and Southern Lakes, the North Coast, Cariboo, Columbia River, Vancouver Island, Lower Mainland, etc. Actually he gives the credit to his granny, Charlotte Roberts, who came out to the coast in 1890 to enjoy her sunset years, thereby launching another of the area's traditions as a retirement area. Granny Roberts, so Harry claimed, first began referring to the little strip of coast around The Creek as "the Sunshine Belt." But Harry it was who undertook to emblazon the slogan in foot-high letters across the wall of the freight shed on the Roberts Creek steamer dock—this was after he'd given up badgering the federal government to build a steamer dock in Roberts Creek, and rallied the local lads to build one themselves.

After Harry decided he'd created a bit of a monster and fled the unbearable hurly-burly of Roberts Creek in 1929, less imaginative promoters continued to exploit his brainwave, changing the arid-sounding "Belt" to the saltier "Coast" and extending its reach until by 1951 when Blackball Ferries linked the Pender Harbour–Gibsons road into the Pacific Coast Highway, the "Sunshine Coast" reached all the way from Port Mellon to Egmont. In recent years it has been something of a surprise to south-enders to look around and discover their northern neighbours on the Powell River side of Jervis Inlet also setting up housekeeping inside the

Some of the last unlogged forest on the Sunshine Coast is located in Spipiyus Provincial Park atop the Caren Range.

Sunshine Coast tent. This unilateral extension of the territory is not without biogeoclimatic justification, as we shall see, but it raises certain questions.

The gerrymandering of BC's provincial electoral districts in 1989 placed the two areas together in one constituency called "Powell River–Sunshine Coast." This would seem to indicate that the provincial government views Powell River and the Sunshine Coast as two separate entities. Indeed, treating them as one immediately creates a new naming problem: how do you distinguish the two quite distinct centres of population from each other? Having to get your mouth around "Upper Sunshine Coast" and "Lower Sunshine Coast" every time you want to evoke Powell River or the original Sunshine Coast complicates life unnecessarily. Powell Riverites have solved the matter to their own satisfaction simply by removing any reference to sunshine from the southern territory and re-dubbing it "The Peninsula" (pronounced pen-**int**-shoe-la). They are not troubled by the geographical fact that only half the area referred to is located on the actual Sechelt Peninsula. Occupants of the lower Sunshine Coast, not eager to be known as a lower form of anything, deal with the problem by ignoring northern pretensions to sunshiny status, invariably referring to any waypoint along the forty-mile stretch between Saltery Bay and Bliss Landing simply as "Powell River." Although it does not seem to have occurred to anyone on the Lower Sunshine Coast Board of Trade, the obvious solution would be to invoke the area's first European explorers, the ones who left such place names as *Texada* Island and *Malaspina* Strait, and replace the English word "lower" with its Spanish equivalent, *baja*, which is free of pejorative undertones. The Baja Sunshine Coast, which local usage would shorten to The Baja, would restore to the southern side a clear lead in the drive for vacationland ambiance.

Even without this recent complication, it would be pointless to deny that the name "Sunshine Coast" has been the target of a certain amount of jeering and ridicule over the years, especially by visitors who inadvertently come to sample the promised sunshine during the monsoon season, which can last from October to May, and has been known to include July and August. The place is located in a temperate rainforest, after all.

Whatever claim to legitimacy the Sunshine name may have, I make a poor champion of it, having once started a publication called *Raincoast Chronicles,* which was quite outspokenly dedicated to projecting a more authentically mist-shrouded, rainswept image for the region. True, geographers have included the original Sunshine Belt, from Gower Point north, in the more benign Gulf Island biogeoclimatic zone (Gibsons was left in the dreary Coastal Western Hemlock zone), but it is clearly on the moist edge of the zone. According to Earl Coatta, a meteorologist at the Atmospheric Environmental Services in Vancouver, the average sunshine total at Merry Island Lightstation off Halfmoon Bay is 1,873 hours per year, slightly better than downtown Vancouver's 1,818 hours, but well below Victoria's 2,185 hours and the provincial high, Cranbrook's 2,229 hours. Precipitation records tell the same tale. Sechelt's average rainfall of 42 inches is closer to Vancouver's 48 inches than Victoria's 25 inches.

Harry Roberts wasn't the only pioneer to woo tourists by trumping up claims of microclimatic anomaly. Forty miles to the west, the Ashworth family attempted to lure unsuspecting customers to the "Royal Savary Hotel," their rustic lodge on Savary Island, by calling it a

Previous pages: Palm Beach near Powell River has no palm trees but plenty of beach. *Darren Robinson*

Opposite: Much of the Sunshine Coast is water access only.

Savary Island's sweeping sandy shores and mild Gulf Island climate have made it a vacationers' paradise.

Savary wharf—private boats and water taxis provide access to the island.

"South Sea Island Paradise." Captain G.J. Ashworth, another backwoods visionary who had much to do with establishing Savary as the coast's busiest summer cottage centre way back in the 1920s, even induced his son, Bill, to greet visitors in a grass skirt and lei, a gimmick that produced mixed results given the younger Ashworth's Ichabod Crane-like physique. On the Powell River shore just a few miles south of Savary, local imagination took an even bolder flight in naming a stretch of sandy shoreline "Palm Beach," later the site of BC's longest running folk festival. Interestingly enough, science lends more credence to the climatic claims of the Ashworth family than those of the Roberts. Just around the corner from Savary, Pendrell Sound on Little Redonda Island has long been known to mariculturists as the only place on the coast where sea water is warm enough to inspire Japanese oysters to spawn on a regular basis. The coastal edge of the Powell River district, from Savary south, shares the same favoured Gulf Island climatic characteristics as the Pender Harbour-to-Gibsons coastline, with one exception. According to *The Atlas of British Columbia*, there is a pinhole in the provincial climatic map that places Savary Island and a fringe of mainland shore from just south of Palm Beach to Desolation Sound as well as Big Redonda Island in a special category that has higher summer temperatures (18-20°C daily mean) than any other part of the BC coast.

LOAFERS AND MUCKERS

BACK IN THE 1980S, BIG AL DAVIDSON (A.K.A. "The Mouth That Roared"), a Vancouver sportscaster who bought the old Cecil Reid place in Pender Harbour, earned himself a black footnote in Sunshine Coast history by announcing on air that the people of the region were nothing but deadbeats and welfare bums. Meaningful glances passed around the waterfront when two charter boats belonging to the pint-sized jock-sniffer went up in flames several months later—and the Mighty Mouth himself was charged with arson. Smug as we felt on that occasion, it must be admitted that Davidson was not the first outlander to be mystified by what appears to be an extensive community just kind of floating in the salt mist with no economic pillars holding it up.

THIS IS LESS THE CASE IN POWELL RIVER, where the smokestacks of what was once the world's largest pulp and paper mill still dominate the skyline, and the Texada skyline just across the strait is terraced by limerock quarries. Down the coast at Port Mellon near Gibsons, Howe Sound Pulp and Paper operates a smaller, more modern pulp mill. Still, between them these two mills only employ about 1,000 people, which leaves about 30,000 voting-age residents unaccounted for. What do they do?

According to the area's economic development offices, about 10 percent of the Sunshine Coast's work force is employed by the forest industry, either as loggers or millworkers. The next largest resource industry is fisheries, a long way back at under 2 percent. The service industries make up by far the largest block of jobs, employing over 60 percent of the work force. This is not necessarily a reflection of tourist activity, which involves only about 15 per-

Many rusting remains attest to the heyday of mechanized logging.

cent. Unemployment is chronically high, hovering in the 10 percent range, and an interesting category headed Not in the labour force is even higher at 39 percent.

I can hear the ghost of Al Davidson drumming its fingers. There's a hell of a lot of people who don't fit readily into any StatsCan job category, I admit, but this still doesn't give credence to the welfare bums rap. I'm afraid the only way to explain is to delve into some abstract metaphysics.

It's true that the Sunshine Coast, by virtue of being an oddball sort of place, attracted oddball sorts of people—but oddballishness is not in itself a very precise category. You can be an oddball by being too fat or too thin, too bright or too dull, too hyper or too sluggish. The motley crew that populated the coast over the past few centuries included examples of all these ilks and more. Even the First Nations had the gentle Dominic Charlie who wished to do nothing but dance, and the psychotic Ts'kahl who would kill you just for being in his way. Later came people like Mac Macdonald, who used gorgeous Princess Louisa Inlet as a stage for expounding his creed of loaferdom, and others like Powell River's non-stop entrepreneur Emil Gordon, who considered the day wasted unless he launched at least one unlikely new enterprise.

But amid all this variety you can discern two broad types, two pioneer strains who can be distinguished from each other by their reason for being on the Sunshine Coast. The first are those who came here for love of the place and were indifferent to the economic prospects, and

Right: A sea lion enjoys the sun at the Powell River booming ground. *Keith Thirkell*

Below: Booms creeping past Halfmoon Bay are a sign of fair weather.

Opposite: Snug harbours and strong salmon runs made the Sunshine Coast the base of a large commercial fishing fleet.

Top: The annual April Fool's Run between Sechelt and Gibsons has been an April tradition since 1978. *Allan Forest*

Bottom: An underwater pumpkin carving contest? Why not! *Allan Forest*

the second are those who came here for economic reasons—to make a living or a fortune—and were indifferent to the *placeness* of the place.

For argument's sake let's use Princess Louisa Mac's term and call the first group the loafers—keeping in mind the fine art of loafing can require a good deal of concerted effort. The second group let's call the muckers, because they tend to be always mucking away at piles of trees or fish or rocks, even though they will tell you the only reason they do it is to get rich enough to retire and enjoy the finer things in life—exactly what the loafers do, except the loafers do it directly and the muckers put it off. Despite this apparent agreement on ultimate aims, you can dip into coast history at any juncture and find the two factions working determinedly at cross-purposes and denouncing each other in the letters columns.

The muckers include most of the loggers and millworkers as well as a good many of the original fishing families, who were brought in to provide labour for the salteries and canneries. They especially include the entrepreneurs and developers, like Herbert Whittaker, who gazed upon the pristine wilderness around Sechelt in 1895 and saw the makings of a private fiefdom, and Thomas Hamilton, the multimillionaire inventor who was so affected by the scenic splendour of Princess Louisa Inlet in 1940 he couldn't rest until he'd devised a way to get it generating revenue.

My family were muckers. We ended up on the coast because my father had the opportunity, back in 1950, to take over a small logging camp at Green Bay on Nelson Island. When that played out he found something else close by. It was an easy place to get by in if you weren't too choosey about what you did, and as the settlements grew Dad operated the area's first sand and gravel business, built one of its first gas stations, and ran the town waterworks. For years we all had the feeling it was an unfortunate accident we had become Sunshine Coasters, figuring if we'd played our cards right we could be in a place with a healthier payroll, like Nanaimo or Campbell River. I was brought up with the impression it was really all happening somewhere else, and if I had any brains I should use them to get away to one of those places at the first opportunity. That was typical of the element who followed jobs to the area. This strain tends to support clearcut logging and wide-open development while showing less concern for the preservation of rural values, although I am living proof that the longer anyone stays, the more his motives tend to get confused.

The loafer tradition was typified by Harry Roberts, who would have fought to the death anybody who tried to push him off his quarter section of paradise on Nelson Island, and by his friend Hubert Evans, the Quaker author of *Mist On The River* and *O Time In Your Flight*, who ended years of questing by settling on an acre of beachfront at Roberts Creek in 1928. Another was Bertrand Sinclair, the high-rolling western writer who cowboyed in Montana and partied on the Barbary Coast before sinking roots at Pender Harbour in 1920. Allen and Sharie Farrell, the coast's ultimate boat people, subsisted for fifty years by squatting on the beach and building exquisite boats from driftwood, living in them for a few years, making the odd crossing to Hawaii or Tahiti, then selling them and building new ones—fifty-two in all. (Allen's son Barrie, as designer of the most popular commercial fishboat hull on the BC coast, was responsible for placing an even greater number of hulls in coastal waters.) People like the Sinclairs, the Macdonalds and the Farrells had seen the world and chose to settle on the Sunshine Coast because its inspiring setting and quiet ways let them get down to the serious business of milking their days here on earth for the most satisfaction possible. Loafing in the Macdonald tradition carries no connotation of laziness, since they could be quite industrious in extracting the manifold satisfactions the coast has to offer. Their heirs tend to be fiercely

protective of the region's traditional qualities, its peaceful country spaces, unspoiled waters and leisurely pace.

In true Sunshine Coast fashion, I'm taking a long time to make a simple point: the type of people described above do not require smokestack industry to survive. They've got the main thing they want in life already—the place of their dreams. For that they are willing to do without a lot of consumer goods considered necessary to life in most of the western world, which allows them to do without the income normally used to buy such goods. My friend Sammy Lamont used to say all he needed to get by was $500 cash for some flour, tea and diesel. This was not back in the dirty thirties, and Sammy was no hermit living in a hollow stump. He and his partner, Ann Clemence, spent the winters in a fine waterfront home in Pender Harbour and the summers cruising the upper coast in their commodious sailboat, the *Kivak*. And no, Sam wasn't landed gentry or a retired banker. He grew up in a cedar shack in the bush behind Powell River and spent most of his working years as a beachcomber salvaging escaped sawlogs. Ann is an ex-nurse trained in England. The two of them didn't want for much. Their furniture was of the finest solid wood construction—all made by Sam himself. They ate well from the sea and from their seaweed-rich vegetable garden, fresh in the summer and put up as preserves in winter. They had tons of friends. They spent their days exploring some of the most dramatic landscape in the world. They lived great lives, and they worked hard for it, but not in a pulp mill. To Statistics Canada they were loafers.

To a greater or lesser degree, many Sunshine Coasters fit the same pattern. This certainly applies to the coast's many artists, writers, musicians and craftspeople, many of whom supplement their sales by working as part-time gardeners, carpenters, marijuana ranchers or bulldozer drivers. Few have achieved such perfect independence as Sam and Ann or Alan and Sharie, but piecing together a livelihood by being handy and living well far below the poverty line is a grand tradition on the Sunshine Coast.

Left: Artist Greta Guzek of Gibsons makes a living selling paintings and cards, and illustrating books.

Above: Abstract painter Motoko combines West Coast and Japanese themes and has a popular studio in Pender Harbour. *Edmond Arceo*

John Pass and Theresa Kishkan are nationally known writers who make their home on Sakinaw Lake near Pender Harbour.

1

THE GIBSONS AREA

WHEN MY DAD AND I RODE on the ceremonial first sailing of the auto ferry across Howe Sound in 1951, we boarded a shimmying cast-off from Puget Sound called the MV *Quillayute*. It docked at the government wharf in Gibsons, which was very handy but caused gridlock in Gibsons' infamous six-way intersection even then. Some years later the ferry corporation revealed its penchant for locating terminae in non-places and relocated the Sunshine Coast base to a desolate stretch of beach near Langdale Creek, four miles north of Gibsons, where it has remained since.

An eagle rests in a shoreside tree as the Langdale ferry plies the waters of Howe Sound.

About 99.9 percent of all the cars unloading at the Langdale dock take the centre and left lanes to Gibsons and points north. The other .1 percent turn right toward Port Mellon. The whole lower ten-mile section of the Sunshine Coast Highway, which is actually set apart with its own name—the Port Mellon Highway—shivers in the shadow of Mount Elphinstone and offers little to the traveller but a view of the coast's industrial underbelly. On the other hand a trip along the Port Mellon Highway goes far toward answering the question about what coast folk do. Along the way you pass the area's last significant sawmill, a played-out gravel pit local government hopes will someday become a busy industrial park, and several of the large "log-sorts" that make Howe Sound the world's largest log booming and sorting ground. About 75 percent of the BC coast's annual 30-million-cubic-metre timber harvest is brought here to be graded, parcelled up and re-shipped to the mills of the Lower Mainland. It is the spillage from this traditional Howe Sound activity that gave rise to the Gibsons area's fabled community of beachcombers, or as they now prefer to be known, "log salvors." The one dramatic event you can sometimes observe along this route is one of the elephantine self-dumping log barges in the act of relieving itself of its load. They come down from up the coast piled high with enough logs to build all the houses in a good-sized town, and flood the bilges on one side, causing the vessel to heel over until the mountain of wood tumbles off and the vessel pops out sideways with a Niagara-like commotion. It is one of the visual cliches of coast life which, like the spawning of the salmon, still makes you catch your breath the first few times you encounter it for real.

At the end of the Port Mellon Highway is Port Mellon, site of BC's longest-surviving pulp and paper mill, established in 1908 by a Victorian adventurer with an admirable flowing beard named Captain Henry Augustus Mellon. The grumpy old salt promptly went broke, but not before he laid one of the foundation stones of the BC economy by successfully producing the province's first sheet of authentic wood-fibre pulp. His erstwhile enterprise eventually revived under different ownership, then went broke again, and continued to stop and start under various owners until being taken over in 1951 by Canadian Forest Products. In 1988 CanFor partnered with Oji Paper of Japan to transform Port Mellon into one of the most modern mills in Canada. Although the upgrade added a newsprint line and doubled the mill's daily output from 500 to 1,000 tons, it cleverly managed to do so without adding

significantly to the existing payroll of some 500 persons—which still makes it the largest single employer on the Baja Sunshine Coast. Visitors to the newly reborn Howe Sound Pulp and Paper expecting to find hordes of brutes massaging the works with six-foot spanners and balancing over burbling vats of bone-melting caustic will be struck by an eerily deserted air about the place. The mighty engines hum robotically along, guided only by scattered pockets of workers slumped at computer terminals in soundproof cubicles equipped with air conditioning and *exercycles*. In 2010 locals were surprised to discover the mill had been sold lock, stock and barrel to Sinar Mas, a multinational based in Indonesia.

At one time Port Mellon supported a substantial company townsite resplendent with restaurant, community hall and even a hotel—the Seaside—located on the banks of the Sunshine Coast's most poetically named watercourse, the Rainy River. The highlight of old Port Mellon's social season was Labour Day, topped off by the crowning of the Pulp Queen. This would be followed by the Pulp Ball, during which numbers of attendees would celebrate by attempting to beat each other to pulp. Most townsite residents made their grateful escape when the road

Left: "The alders are the re-occupiers, the forestfixers…" —Peter Trower, "The Alders."

Above: A barge unloads in Howe Sound. Howe Sound carries on a long tradition of serving as the log-sorting capital of the BC coast.

31

Left: Who says wildlife and industry don't mix? A barred owl snoozes through the loading of a pulp ship at Port Mellon.

Below: Being the capital of log sorting also made Howe Sound the capital of log salvaging as beachcombers feasted on the spillage.

Opposite: While other BC coast pulp mills have closed, the one at Port Mellon continues to be the largest employer on the Baja Sunshine Coast.

Opposite: Hopkins Landing, adjacent to the Langdale Ferry Terminal, is still occupied by some of the original Hopkins family.

was punched through to Gibsons in 1954, but the company kept some houses in service for new arrivals and management until the early 1980s. The last of these was demolished in 1988, leaving only the renegade private townsite half a mile west of the mill, still officially known to the world as Dogpatch.

Masochists who take this less travelled road may be overcome by the gloom of the landscape and despair for people who voluntarily accept life sentences to such purgatorial surroundings. I have often harboured similar thoughts, passing through industrial backwaters like Aberdeen, Washington—but to do so is to presume too much. Just as the soot-caked rowhouses of Nottingham produced one of the century's most visionary glorifiers of the sheer joy of living in D.H. Lawrence, and Aberdeen gave birth to the rock prophet Kurt Cobain, bleak Port Mellon will long be remarked as the gestation-place of Peter Trower, the poetic genius who penned such inspirational anthems to coastal existence as "The Alders" and "Along Green Tunnels." In his poem "When The Mill Was Our Mother" Trower reveals a bit of what old Port Mellon felt like to the inmates:

When the mill was our mother...
an uncouth mother
of belching stacks and old machinery...
who deeded us a town to live in
tumbledown without pretensions
on the rainy river's brink
full of tarpaper palaces
with pulp-lined interiors
full of simple caring people...
Like one family we lived...
in that kingdom of friendly destiny
we had nothing we had everything

Battling depression brought on by industrial squalor wherever it's found, it can be useful to think of Pete and his comrades taking sulfurous succour from the old Port Mellon mill, keeping the flame burning perhaps a little brighter against the gloom of their surroundings.

Working on the boomsticks, Howe Sound.

THE 99.9 PERCENT who resist the urge to turn right coming off the ferry need not trouble themselves with such existential perplexities. The three-mile drive into Gibsons Landing passes above some of the better beaches on the lower coast—most of them used only by the choice waterfront homes that front them, although there are some well-concealed public access points. The whole of the lower Sunshine Coast, including Gambier and Keats islands, Sechelt Inlet and Jervis Inlet, is infested with summer camps; the YMCA, the Boy Scouts, the Girl Guides, and every church in the phone book have nice spreads. One of the humbler installations, the Salvation Army's Camp Sunrise, can be seen from the highway just past the Langdale ferry terminal.

Before reaching Gibsons Landing the traveller passes two lesser landings, Hopkins and

Granthams. Most people who don't live there can't tell you which is which, so remember: Hopkins is just a hop from the ferry and the two G-landings, Granthams and Gibsons, are side by side at the farther end of the twisty little drive. What is noteworthy about these communities including the part of Gibsons nearest them is how many of the older structures—the original Mansard-roofed Granthams store as well as the millworkers' bungalows, summer cottages and many of the sagging commercial buildings of the old First War Gibsons core—have managed to survive, preserving the quaint old fishing village flavour that has made Gibsons such a favourite among Sunday painters and calendar publishers, not to mention the movie industry. It's a minor miracle which must have the town's condo developers wondering what they did wrong.

When Philip Keatley, the Canadian Broadcasting Corporation producer who originated the *Beachcombers* TV series, phoned me for advice on where to find a coastal village authentic enough to serve as the location for the show, I spoke against Gibsons because I thought the original look of the place was too far gone even then, way back in the early 1970s. I told him he should take his show up the road to Egmont, which was a more unspoiled example of the traditional BC fishing village. A lot of people have reason to be grateful he ignored my counsel, since the *Beachcombers*, filmed in Gibsons, went on to enjoy a nineteen-year run as the most successful television drama ever produced in Canada, while a later show called *Ritter's Cove*, which Keatley did locate in Egmont, bombed after a few seasons.

Even though the last *Beachcombers* episode was filmed in 1992, reruns perpetuate it almost everywhere except Canada. Some first-time visitors still steam up their windscreens and lose control of their Winnebagos as they swing into lower Gibsons and without any warning find themselves smack in the middle of the hallowed *Beachcombers* set.

"Good gawd, Martha, look! There's Molly's Reach right there staring at us!"

"And Smitty's marina over there!"

"Hey Mom, I think I see the *Persephone*!"

"Can we stop and look, Daddy? Puh-leeeze!"

What is especially beguiling to visitors is that the town itself does so little to advertise or acknowledge its connection to TV-land, leaving them to discover it on their own—if they can find a place to park the camper without coming to grief in the coast's most accident-prone six-way intersection. All summer long you can find tourists peering with cupped hands through the windows of the old liquor store, which the CBC turned into a stage cafe known to millions as Molly's Reach. For many years, the most interesting thing to be seen in the false-fronted old store was a prodigious display of rat droppings.

One summer an enterprising type tried to set up a real-life cafe offering Molly's famous homemade pie and the Relic Special (ketchup on everything), set off with a display of *Beachcombers* memorabilia, but the village wouldn't give her a parking permit for the vacant Reach. Harry Smith, the owner of the building, tried to start a restaurant on the premises again in 1995. The town council responded by saying they didn't want to be rushed into anything, before finally bowing to public outrage and backing down. In a fine example of life imitating art the business took off and by the 2010s the landmark was firmly established as something it had never really been before—a real-life restaurant. In the first edition of this book I wrote, "Any other town would have bronzed the *Persephone*, the beachcombing tug operated by series hero Nick Adonidas (played by the late Bruno Gerussi), and mounted it in Pioneer Square, surrounded by fibreglass replicas of the entire Beachcomber cast, but Gibsons shrugs and goes about its life, glad the traffic stoppages caused by outdoor shooting are finally over."

Helen, freelance bottle-and-can collector, is a familiar friendly face in Gibsons.

Opposite top: Lower Gibsons in early spring.

Opposite bottom: Life imitates art. After having served nineteen years as a fictional eatery for the popular TV series *The Beachcombers*, Molly's Reach was turned into a real restaurant.

Well, somebody must have been paying attention because in the decade since, city authorities did dig the *Persephone* out of its blackberry patch and mount it at the intersection—not bronzed, but nicely painted up.

Clearly, this town of 6,000 is not about to be swept off its feet by a little cinematic glitter. On the contrary, the longer the series went on, the more the CBC seemed to fall under the influence of Gibsons. After living in the village for several seasons the film cowboys began to realize the life around them offered much richer material than the cheesy fantasies they parachuted in from Toronto, and began producing episodes more reflective of actual coastal experience. Locals hired as go-fers and extras gradually took on more important roles, like my old DeMolay brother Johnny Smith, a real-life beachcomber who went from boat handler to director, and is now jet-setting around the globe as a film producer. Others, like Gerussi, downshifted from the fast lane to stay on as permanent Sunshine Coast residents, abetted not a little by the booty from nineteen years of pretend beachcombing. Legend has it the mighty Nick piloted the *Persephone* through a generation of high-seas highjinks twisting on a helm that wasn't actually connected to anything, the real operator huddling out of view in the bilge. Largely as a result of the long run of the *Beachcombers*, the Gibsons–Roberts Creek area has a higher concentration of retired and semi-retired film types than any precinct north of Marin County. It has also served as the setting for Stephen King's horror film *Needful Things,* the film version of L.R. Wright's Sechelt murder mystery *The Suspect* and a number of other films.

This is what I like about Gibsons. It has a long history of seriousness which it is not about to toss away just to become a world-famous movie capital. It has its feet planted firmly on the ground., like the bronze statue of its founder in Pioneer Square. It would be hard to think of a more serious individual than old George Gibson with his sad baggy eyes and stooping shoulders, looking as if the weight of the world were eternally upon them.

Like George Gibson, who came to the coast after a career as a British naval officer, many early settlers of the Howe Sound area were staid WASPs on the verge of retirement. George Hopkins, who in 1906 bought the 160-acre site that would become Hopkins Landing, was a British engineer who'd sold his Swansea boiler works for health reasons. George Grantham of Granthams Landing was an eminent Vancouver businessman who bought 800 feet of waterfront on Howe Sound because he wanted someplace to stick a summer cabin and in 1909 that was the smallest parcel he could buy. He never actually lived full-time at the village that took his name.

These first-comers manifested some behaviourisms that present-day residents probably consider unique to their own times. Many of them came from the city seeking escape and many subsequently found it necessary, as Lester Peterson remarked in *The Gibsons Landing Story*, to "shuttle back and forth between West Howe Sound and Vancouver, seeking employment in Vancouver to keep the wolf from the door at home." The founders no doubt viewed this survival tactic as a temporary measure soon to be eliminated by an expanding local economy. They might be surprised to return today and see the vast battalion of commuters hugging insulated mugs and massaging laptops as they wait to pile aboard the 6:20 ferry at Langdale each morning.

When the enterprising F.C. Grantham began laying water pipes and surveying his 800 feet of paradise into small lots five years before the First World War, he probably didn't realize he was trailblazing a subdividing and selling impulse that would preoccupy peninsula people increasingly for the rest of the century. Sometimes it seems as if every other tree on the Sunshine Coast has a For Sale sign on it, and few are the residents who haven't traded property up,

The Annual Sea Cavalcade celebrates Gibsons' saltwater connection. *Allan Forest*

Opposite: Gibsons from the air.

down or sideways at least once. Some properties have been bought and sold so many times it is claimed they've generated more in sales commissions than they're worth to buy.

An event transpired in 1905 that greatly aided Gibsons' development as a community although it did nothing to relieve the prevailing climate of seriousness. This was the arrival of the Finns. BC had the privilege of hosting many pioneer immigrants from Finland, and they were not always noted for taking part in mainstream community life, but the Gibsons Finns were different. These families, the Katos, the Wilanders, the Ruises, the Hintsas, the Lantas, the Sauris, and the Wirens, were refugees from a failed socialist Utopia called Sointula, founded in 1901 on Malcolm Island, 150 miles north up the Inside Passage. Having the agricultural bent of most Old Country folk, the Finns were drawn to the flat land on the bench behind the Gibsons waterfront. There they laboriously cleared most of the open fields which remained until lately as a prominent feature of the area known as Gibsons Heights. Driving through Gibsons Heights today you can tell the Finnish homesteads from the habit their founders had of placing buildings back in the middle of the property rather than at the edge nearest the road. A dwindling number of old farmhouses still stand well back from the highway in the midst of large fields.

Liz Williams' lush houseboat garden in Gibsons delights locals and visitors alike.
Christina Symons

As Socialist Utopians, these Finnish settlers had community building in the blood. They immediately set about organizing their new neighbours, erecting the first community hall, the first post office, a co-op store, and a co-op jam cannery for processing the berries, which turned out to be the only thing that the poor glacial soils of Gibsons Heights produced on a commercial scale.

The Finns were veteran political campaigners and brought their radical leftist beliefs to bear on all community issues from education to medical care to religion. The WASP old guard, led by storekeeper Harry Winn, were thoroughly scandalized by the rabble-rousing foreigners and mounted a heated defence of God and the King that made Gibsons a hotbed of political debate that still echoes down the corridors of time.

What is noteworthy is how successful the Finns were in bringing many of the other settlers around to their views. They found a staunch ally in the community doctor, Frederick Inglis, who in turn did his best to indoctrinate the local Methodist minister. The minister, who was struggling to square the pro-war position of the church with his own pacifist leanings, proved receptive enough to the radical talk to get himself fired by the local parish, whereupon he was forced to move his entire family into the doctor's house above the Gibsons wharf. In those close quarters the dialectic intensified, with the minister struggling to find a middle path between the firebrands up on the flats and the flag-waving mossbacks down on the Gibsons waterfront. The position he hammered out changed the course of Canadian history. The minister's name was James Shaver Woodsworth and he went on to found the most successful political party of the left in North America, a democratic-socialist hybrid of capitalism and socialism called the Co-operative Commonwealth Federation (CCF), later the New Democratic Party (NDP). In 2011, the NDP formed two of Canada's provincial governments as well as the official opposition in Ottawa, although the old CCF spirit in Gibsons had been somewhat diluted by waves of well-heeled retirees fleeing the Lower Mainland.

The house in which the founder of the CCF did his soul-searching still stands opposite Molly's Reach and surely deserves protection as one of the historic landmarks of Gibsons if not of Canada, but village authorities have so far passed up all opportunities to acquire it.

It may be a bit of a romantic conceit nowadays with all the strip mall and condo development up the hill, but I have always felt Gibsons' centre of gravity is the part the city fathers tried to deep-six back in 1947, namely the landing. All BC coast communities, from Vancouver to Prince Rupert, are growing away from the working waterfronts that gave them their original reason for being, but Gibsons' small-boat harbour remains busy and viable, supporting a handful of marinas, several shipyards, and one of the best government wharves left on the BC coast.

The red-railed government wharf, a sturdy, centrally located, well-maintained timber-and-piling dock provided by the federal Department of Transport (now the local harbour authority), has over the years been the most important public institution in every seafront village on the BC coast. In places without road access, the government wharf was where the steamers and larger freight vessels made their all-important landing on "boat day," as much a social as a working occasion, when all and sundry would gather on the foot-polished plank deck to visit, whether they had any boat business or not. The "guvermint worf" was the coast town's Piccadilly Circus and Times Square, where all the joyous arrivals and sad departures took place. Many government wharves have been downsized to eliminate their steamship-docking capacity, or eliminated by neoconservative political regimes anxious to disable all truly effective government services, but Gibsons remains one of the few that can still accommodate a sea-going ship as well as a ragtag population of old wooden tugs, ex-North Sea trawlers, evil-looking log salvage jet boats, rickety live-aboards, half-sunken hulks and other vessels of character, reputable and otherwise.

Gibsons' small-boat harbour makes for a fascinating dock walk.

41

Top: With its multitude of islands, safe harbours and fair winds, the entire Sunshine Coast is a yachters' dream.

Right: Gibsons' working waterfront bears witness to its maritime heritage.

Boats are central to the lives of island people and near-island people. Aboriginal life on the Sunshine Coast was made possible by the existence of the ubiquitous cedar dugout, and the first wave of non-Native pioneers such as the Roberts Creek Robertses paddled their possessions ashore in large clinker-built rowboats purchased in Vancouver from a transplanted Bluenose boatbuilder named Andy Linton. Settlement didn't kick into high gear until a regular steamer connection with Vancouver was established by the Union Steamship Company in 1888, and ships of that company like the *Comox, Cowichan, Chelohsin* and *Capilano* play the kind of role in Sunshine Coast history that the Mardi Gras plays in the history of New Orleans, as in, "I met my first husband on the *Cowichan*, but then I lost him on the *Cynthia*."

When I cast backward for my first memory of the Sunshine Coast, what I come up with is a boat. A fifty-foot fish packer named the *Murpak I*, which my father had hired on May 24, 1950, to move my mother, me, my two sisters and our worldly belongings from Vancouver to our new logging camp home on Nelson Island. There is an undertone of unhappiness to the memory—of overstressed parents barking orders unnecessarily harsh, of my baby sister greeting the strangeness with six hours of inconsolable howling, of my own deep insecurities about leaving the known world behind—but laid over this is the memory of adventure, the unexpected thrill of sailing off in the brave ship *Murpak I*.

Marking the years since are more memories of boats and trips on boats—the ex-rum-runner *Suez*, our leaky old camp tender that I piloted home through a foaming middle-of-the-night gale at age nine because the crew who invited me to come along on the weekly grocery run to Pender Harbour were too drunk to stand, let alone steer. The *Jervis Express*, an ex-World War II sub chaser doing ungainly service as a passenger freighter, bringing our Christmas presents up from Vancouver two weeks late and soaking wet. The *Flash*, the backyard cabin cruiser my father built to fulfill his dream of owning the perfect boat, but which rotted on blocks without ever getting quite finished.

Fishing families in Pender Harbour mark off the periods of their lives not by births, deaths or natural catastrophes but according to the boats they owned at the time, as in, "It must have been before February 13, 1946, that Ma run off because that's when I got the *Okeefenokee Queen* and when she was here I still had the *Sea Bag*."

People even refer to each other by the names of their boats sometimes: "You're *Sea Aggressor*? I'm *Lonesome Polecat*. You corked me last August in Bear Bight!"

In modern times much of the boat life of the Sunshine Coast has been sacrificed to the Age of the Automobile, but road travel is still ultimately dependent on the ships of the BC Ferry Corporation, and no news will move up the seaweed telegraph faster than word the "*Cow*" (*Queen of Cowichan*) has ripped out the Langdale dock again, or the *Island Sky* is running an hour behind schedule because somebody jumped overboard on the 4:30 run. People wouldn't consider getting married on the BC Ferries like they did on the "Union boats," but they remain an important social institution nonetheless. I sometimes feel I would lose touch with my neighbours completely if I didn't keep running into them on the ferry.

The boats at the government wharf in Gibsons are the boats of the coast's real boat people, and a visitor can learn more about the authentic maritime culture of the region in a half-hour dock walk there than in weeks of haunting museums. With luck, she can also negotiate a good deal on some live-landed Howe Sound prawn or halibut from the hold of a longliner fresh in from Haida Gwaii. The Whiskey Slough float in Pender Harbour also shelters a handsome collection of commercial work boats and the government docks at Westview and Lund harbour smaller communities of working wharf rats, but not on the scale of Gibsons.

Some far-sighted early planner provided Gibsons with a waterfront esplanade that has recently been opened up to Sunday strollers, and this twenty-minute walk makes a great way to visit the Sunshine Coast's most famous stretch of beach. If you plan your hike from north to south you will come out just a crooked block from the Elphinstone Pioneer Museum at Gower Point and Gower Point, one of the better small-town museums you'll find.

Many visitors to the Sunshine Coast drive the entire hundred miles of the Sunshine Coast Highway never having really seen much actual sea coast and wondering why. One answer would be that nobody in a position to do so ever thought to make allowances for visitors who might want to get down to the water, or see more than the odd glimpse of it. But another answer is that there are some well-concealed points of access where one can slip off the highway and inhale a bit of seaweed-scented breeze if you know where to go. One of the nicest is out at the end of Gower Point Road where it turns into Ocean Beach Esplanade. Gower Point is itself one of the older settlements in the area, although it is quite distinct in character, having a long history as a summer cabin centre for vacationing Vancouverites. A lovely little provincial park, complete with a cairn commemorating Captain Vancouver's brief stopover in 1792, rests right at the water's edge by the mouth of Chaster Creek. The cobble beach is not for bare feet and the water is icy even in August, but there is no better place on the coast to barbecue a cob of corn and watch the sun explode in salmons and corals as it squelches its flames in the sea beyond Lasqueti Island.

Above: Fraser Blues precision flyers soar above the crowds at Gibsons Sea Cavalcade. *Allan Forest*

Right: A winning float in the Gibsons Sea Cavalcade. *Allan Forest*

ROBERTS CREEK

IF YOU FOLLOW GOWER POINT ROAD TO where it turns into Ocean Beach Esplanade and then follow Ocean Beach to where it dead-ends in the brush, you have gone as far north as you can and still be said to be in greater Gibsons. One further step and you enter into the domain of Roberts Creek. Roberts Creek is a diffuse, five-mile stretch of coast reaching from Gower Point to Wilson Creek. It is so formless geographically the casual visitor might make the mistake of thinking it is not really a community at all, merely surplus territory waiting to be used up by Gibsons and Sechelt sprawl.

Upon meeting any one of the 3,307 Creekers who occupy the territory any such impression would be quickly dispelled. There is no community on the Gulf with a more defiant sense of its own sovereignty. "The Creek" is a state of mind as much as a place, and the mind is as different from the serious, shift-working mind of Gibsons as the puckish spirit Harry Roberts is from the dour, sad ghost of George Gibson. Where Gibsons favours ex-business types for mayor, the Creek's regional director all through the 1980s and '90s was a bearded geography prof who lived in a solar house and built a bureaucratic barricade aimed at holding Sechelt and Gibsons sprawl at bay.

Roberts Creek is the Sunshine Coast's Haight-Ashbury, the place where the rebel consciousness of the 1960s found its most fertile ground and achieved its most extreme expression.

Equine traffic pauses to take in the autumn colours in downtown Roberts Creek.
Keith Thirkell

Right: Roberts Creek residents let out their inner Creeker at Creek Daze. *Allan Forest*

Below: Robert Van Norman, founder of the Inside Passage School of Fine Cabinetmaking in Roberts Creek.

Below right: Kim La Fave started a successful illustrating career in Toronto, which he keeps up via internet from his studio in Roberts Creek.

Author Ken Drushka, who spent the summer of 1968 giving out government Opportunities For Youth grants to people who wanted to start communes, once told me he found as many eager applicants in Roberts Creek as in the whole rest of the province. But Creek elders like Doug and Helen Roy would say that the roots of back-to-the-land thinking go much deeper, and have lasted much longer as a consequence. In the book, *Remembering Roberts Creek*, Hubert Evans, who chucked the life of a downtown media celebrity for Creek existence back in 1927, remembered the incident that made up his mind, way back then:

In 1927 a couple seeking less-hurried lifestyles than they had found in cities visited Roberts Creek. During a stroll they stopped to watch an elderly man fastening wire claws to the end of a long cedar pole he had shaped. "For hooking up mussels, the big ones low down on the wharf piles," the man explained.

"Mussels for eating?"

"For catching shiners. Shiners make good cod bait. I aim to go cod fishing the day after." Three unhurried days to catch a cod! Then and there the couple knew their search had ended.

HUBERT MOVED HIS FAMILY onto an acre of waterfront at the mouth of Stephens Creek and soon became an adept in the Creek lifestyle, writing assiduously until sales of his stories for children's magazines totalled $2,500 for the year. At that point he would purposefully down his pen and take the rest of the year off, cruising up and down the coast with his family in their 28-foot gasboat, the *Solheim*. When the latter-day wave of back-to-the-landers rolled around four decades later, Hubert was able to view them with some bemusement in his poem, "Flower Children":

Above: Sculptor Scott Avery created this unusual bench using a remnant from the late Ray Jenkins' sculpture, "The Whale," which once graced the Roberts Creek pier but was cut down by vandals. *Allan Forest*

Below: Sunset at the mouth of Roberts Creek.

Old pilings bear witness to busier times in the Roberts Creek estuary.

They came starry-eyed from the city
to walk with nature
But only to her chosen
would she give her hand.

Evans' and Roberts' nonconformist, artistic, nature-loving spirits live on in the modern community, which includes the highest concentration of painters, musicians, potters, writers, homespun philosophers and ornery stump ranchers of any place on the coast.

The creek mouth, where Harry Roberts built the first store and community wharf, is still the nearest thing Roberts Creek has to a downtown, with a store, post office, school, Legion, several eateries, a boutique mall and just up the road a firehall and a venerable old community hall. What it doesn't have any longer is a functioning wharf or any vestige of the busy harbour Harry Roberts developed back in the 1920s. Above the highway as well as below, the Creek's sloping south-facing sea exposure makes it a perfect theatre from which to contemplate the beauties of Georgia Strait, but modern Creekers are a landlubberly lot compared to their neighbours in Gibsons and Pender Harbour. Their geography leaves little choice. Among boaters, the shoreline from Gower Point north is known as "the Stretch," a harbourless gauntlet one must run between Gibsons and the shelter of the Trail Islands off Sechelt. Evans reflected on the ironies of Creekers' relationship to the sea in his poem, "Unrequited Love":

"I love the sea," she tells me.
Well and good, dear lady,

but let me caution you
the sea will not reciprocate.
During my years here
within sight of this house
the following have drowned:

1 settler
4 towboat men
3 heedless boys
3 youthful canoeists
3 fishermen
1 toddler
1 bride-to-have-been
As indicated by the foregoing
the sea is not selective.
It does not play favourites.
Unlike Jehovah it has no chosen people.

As compensation for its pitiless lack of shelter, the Roberts Creek shore offers some of the coast's better beaches, though once again they're easy to miss from the highway. MacFarlane's Beach is a crescent of gravel and soft sand just downstream from the creek mouth which can be accessed from the old wharf right-of-way at the foot of Roberts Creek Road (now a regional

Top: The little park at the foot of Flume Road is a popular swimming beach.

Bottom: Wave-sculpted beach rocks, Roberts Creek.

Above: The Dakota Ridge recreation area gives
Sunshine Coast recreation a winter dimension.
Allan Forest

Left: The towering bulk of Mount Ephinstone
dominates the lower Sunshine Coast.
Keith Thirkell

Above: Black bears and people co-exist in relative peace at Roberts Creek.

Right: A moss-covered cabin bears silent witness to a homesteader's struggle in the backcountry running up the flanks of Mount Elphinstone.

park), and there is another stretch of pebbles punctuated by massive wave-sculpted boulders at the tiny provincial park at the foot of Flume Road.

The Creek also boasts perhaps the most hospitable upland area on the Sunshine Coast, with thousands of acres of flattish land sloping gently back from the beach and on up the foot of Mount Elphinstone. Much of this land was cleared in the early part of the century by eager homesteaders who soon found the sad truth about the thin, acidic soil that underlays coniferous forests, and gave up farming for the more lucrative alternative of logging.

Poor as it is for food crops, the soil of the Sunshine Coast is one of the most outstanding timber growing sites on the planet and its original Douglas-fir forest was one of the wonders of the natural world. On the north end of the Sechelt Peninsula it gave rise to larger-scale railroad logging operations but some of the best timber on the lower end was destroyed in 1906 by a promethean forest fire that started in the area of the Boy Scout camp and thundered across the western face of Mount Elphinstone almost as far as Howe Sound. Miles of prime timber were reduced to skeletal snags and the ash in places was said to be ten feet deep. In dry winds it drifted like snow in a prairie blizzard.

The area eventually reseeded itself, with the result that today the lower slopes of Mount

Elphinstone support one of the most densely stocked second-growth fir forests in the province, now actively being re-logged. This has not escaped the notice of the environment-conscious denizens of Roberts Creek, who have launched a spirited campaign to save the young forest from clear-cutting by the major forest companies. Instead they are urging it be preserved or else selectively logged by small tenure holders like the late Tom Wright and his son, Bill, two local woodlot operators whose Witherby Tree Farm has been quietly proving for half a century that small can be beautiful in the BC woods.

It was the old overgrown stump ranches left behind by the early homesteaders-turned-loggers that were discovered by delighted commune-seekers in the 1960s. Crowe Road alone was once said to be the home of a dozen of these groups, and legend has it somewhere back in the bush one still endures. The jungles behind Roberts Creek are also reputed to conceal some 1960s refugees who, when all the hair fell out, were revealed to be scions of famous and wealthy families, and established comfortable estates with their inheritances. Yuppies hungering for the rural ambiance are squeezing out the last of the Creek's unreformed Age of Aquarius survivors, but the woods still harbour a few of the classic old tarpaper palaces strewn about with fabulous collections of junk. Perhaps there are still even a few marijuana-ranching

Standing dead trees or snags play an important part in the mature rainforest.

53

Top: Larger whales such as this gray photographed from Davis Bay, once rarely seen, are returning to coastal waters. *Allan Forest*

Bottom: Davis Bay has one of the more expansive sand beaches on the lower coast, as well as the best stretch of ocean-view driving. *Allan Forest*

Right: The Davis Bay wharf, one of several left over from the days of steamboat travel, is now used for sightseeing and fishing.

operations. The drug trade was for some time Roberts Creek's most conspicuous economic activity, and in the 1970s and 1980s it was not uncommon for local papers to carry accounts of drug-related beatings and shootings. Now it seems the business has either died down or established more traditional methods of credit management.

DRIVING NORTH ON THE HIGHWAY, IT'S NOT hard to tell where the influence of the Roberts Creek nature-lovers ends—at the point where the strip malls start back up again, just across the border between Roberts Creek District and Sechelt Municipality at Wilson Creek. Wilson Creek, Davis Bay and Selma Park form a generally unbroken continuum of subdivisions the rest of the way into Sechelt proper. The most notable feature is the stretch of oceanview motoring at Davis Bay where the highway fronts the shoreline of the bay. For many visitors this is the scenic highlight of their trip, the only good taste of open seascape they get on the much-touted scenic drive up the Sunshine Coast.

When you have spent your entire life in a place, certain locations come to have special meaning, and for me this is one. Forty years ago the gravel spit that juts out into Georgia Strait off Chapman Creek almost made me an orphan. Just before our family moved to the isolated camp in Green Bay that became our first Sunshine Coast home, my father was charged with the task of transferring the rickety camp tender *Suez* from Vancouver to Green Bay. All went well until he challenged the dreaded "Stretch," the exposed thirty-mile section of open gulf between Howe Sound and Sechelt. A big southeaster blew up and at the crucial moment, as Dad was straining to round the tide-whipped spit at Mission Point, the old Chrysler Crown sputtered to a stop. He tried every trick in the book to restart it, but to no avail. There are not too many places on the shores of Georgia Strait where surf can be said to actually break, but Mission Point in a big southeaster is one. Dad fought as long as he could to keep the punky old rumrunner clear of the thundering surf with a pike pole, then he bailed over the side, planted himself firmly in the gravel of Mission Spit and personally held the heaving ten-ton vessel off the shore all night. In daylight he poled the derelict over to the Davis Bay wharf and staggered in to the then Selma Park Lodge. The suspicious manager was barely persuaded to admit him to a room where he convulsed with hypothermia for twenty-four hours, passing in and out

Sunshine Coast polar bear cubs get ready to welcome the New Year with an icy dip. *Allan Forest*

Boat Day at Selma Park. *Sunshine Coast Museum & Archive, 1050*

of consciousness. Then he went down to the boat, cleaned the caked salt off all the ignition wires and proceeded to Green Bay where he found everyone wondering what had taken him so long. He often told me that night on Mission Point was a kind of turning point, where he started out a feisty young buck who thought he could face any physical challenge, but came away a sadder and wiser adult who realized he had limits. He also felt that in that one stormy night he had broken his health, which had been flawless until then but never after. My sympathy is tempered by the fact that as the second edition of this book came out in 2011, he was still sneaking out for the odd joy-ride at age 97.

I experienced my own brush with hypothermia at Davis Bay when I somehow got inveigled into trying my luck in the annual Polar Bear swim, some fifty years after Dad spent his night holding the *Suez* off the frigid winter waters of Mission Point. I managed the compulsory fifteen minutes, but was speechless with shock for the next six hours. They just don't make 'em like they used to.

Chilly as the water often is even in mid-summer, Davis Bay is still the most popular beach on the Baja, the site of a sometime sand castle contest that draws thousands and reduces through-traffic on the Sunshine Coast's main artery to a crawl all day. The old wharf is the last of the three steamer docks that used to offer relief to boaters navigating the Stretch, although nowadays it is only used by strollers and sport fishers. Long the site of an annual Charlie Brookman Fishing Derby for kids, the wharf has a faithful year-round clientele of sport fishermen, who still manage to catch the odd fish.

For the fisherman who knows his business, there are salmon to be had along the Davis Bay shore.

2
THE SECHELT AREA

IF PRESENT-DAY ROBERTS Creek seems to carry on with the non-conforming, spiritual style of Harry Roberts, present-day Sechelt might be said to carry on in the mercantile, entrepreneurial manner of Herbert Whittaker. Whittaker was no more the founder of Sechelt than Roberts was of Roberts Creek, but he was just as much the guy who put it on the map. A mere stripling of eighteen when he arrived in Sechelt with his father, Alfred, in 1893, Whittaker was up to his elbows in land development within two years, subdividing the old Scales preemption into the original Sechelt townsite. Young Whittaker was a whirling dervish of commercial enterprise. By the time he was twenty-two he'd put up a twenty-one-room hotel, a store and a post office, and before he was done he would own two more hotels, a much larger store, a row of rental houses, a dance hall, a couple of sawmills, five logging camps, two commercial wharves and two steamship lines. Did I mention a farm? He also may have been the first full-time resident of the Sunshine Coast to own a motor vessel that existed solely to provide its owner with pleasure, a cabin cruiser called the *Resort*. He was the coast's first tycoon—and its first bankrupt tycoon. In 1924, following a period of illness, he lost his property to the bank, where the Union Steamship Company picked it up cheap and continued to promote Sechelt as a resort village.

Previous pages: Sechelt's most striking feature is the narrow isthmus it occupies.

Sechelt rivals Roberts Creek in its magnificent sweep of south-facing waterfront on Trail Bay, but since the old steamer wharf was dismantled and replaced with a pedestrian pier, public use has pretty much been limited to enjoying the view and loading gravel from the big loading facility in front of the reserve. From a quarter-mile out, the sweeping crescent of white beach looks so inviting you wonder why it's not speckled with bathers, but closer inspection reveals egg-sized cobbles that make for more of a foot massage than most people want on their days off, and the three-knot current keeps the water temperature too bracing for comfort in

Snicket Park faces the open seas of Georgia Strait. *Keith Thirkell*

anything but scorching weather. Still, the beachfront "Boulevard" which begins just west of the historic Sechelt Indian Reserve No. 2 on Wharf and runs west to Ocean Avenue, makes a rewarding five-minute walk, especially if you continue up to tiny but exquisite Snicket Park at the westward end, where the wave-polished granite ramparts do invite bare feet. From the 1920s until the 1950s, this bumpy stretch of wagon path was Sechelt's main street, giving access to two hotels, three general stores, a post office, a school, some houses and a row of rental cabins. Highlighted by the totem poles beside the first general store, it presented an impressive facade to anyone approaching the town by sea, which hundreds of picnickers did aboard Whittaker's steamers the *Tartar* and the *Sechelt*. The little town was regularly swamped with low-budget holidayers off work from Vancouver factories and offices, as Sam Dawe, skipper of the *Tartar*, remembered in *Helen Dawe's Sechelt*.

In those days before prohibition the hotel boasted a very fine bar with a view over the straits. Inasmuch as Mr. Whittaker at one time operated five logging camps and some shingle-bolting camps in or near Sechelt Inlet, at times it became somewhat rowdy...the attempt to mix tourism with loggers was not always too successful.

One building from this era remained into 2011, a clapboard bungalow with serpentine roofline known as the Green Cottage, built as a tourist rental in the 1920s. The last time I was in one of these cottages it was occupied by the writer Hajo Hadeler and the structure was so warped by time and uncertain foundations that whenever his little boy, Jason, let go of his toy truck it would go careening across the floor and fetch up against the wall on the low side of

Gravel mining is one of Sechelt's leading employers.
Allan Forest

61

the room. That particular cottage, nicknamed Kwicherkickin, eventually crumbled into the ground, but I am happy to report Jason has grown into a strapping young man who was driving a real truck the last time I saw him.

There are few better ways to spend your time in Sechelt than to amble along this historic boulevard, pick out a nice beach log to sit on, and take in the view across the expanse of BC's great inland sea, which is here at its broadest point. If you have your birding glasses you may be able to pick out humungous sea lions sunning themselves on the reef between Trail Island No. 2 and Trail Island No. 3. My father also instructed me on an infallible method of reading weather signs from this charmed location, which I am now prepared to reveal publicly for the first time. If wind is coming, you will see a whole pile of tugboats with log booms all clustered in behind the Trail Islands. This is the last shelter before the Stretch and the tugs won't pass by unless they've heard on their radios there's enough calm weather for them to run the gauntlet down into Howe Sound or the Fraser River. So if you see tugs with booms parading by, it means at least six hours before any serious wind.

Opposite: A Sechelt totem looks out over Trail Islands and the broad expanse of the Strait of Georgia.

Sechelt's most striking physical feature is the narrow isthmus it occupies, which from the height of a passing float plane seems barely sufficient to hold the outer waters of Georgia Strait apart from the 100 miles of landlocked shoreline comprising Sechelt, Narrows and Salmon inlets. Providing access between these two waterways has long been identified as one of the chief advantages of the site. Legend has it the shíshálh were the first to try digging a canal through the sandy soil of the isthmus, which might have made sense in pre-smallpox times when the inner waters were more heavily settled than the outer ones. The canal brainwave has ebbed and flowed over the years, most recently in the 1980s when then Mayor Bud Koch became noisily possessed of the notion, but the problem has always been that not that many people really need a $40-million canal in order to take small craft from the Gulf into Sechelt Inlet. Logging activity in the inlet has dwindled to a handful of stragglers, and apart from a few fish farmers there is virtually nobody living year-round beyond the Porpoise Bay–Tuwanek area. The last of the old Inlet dwellers was a solitary trapper and woodsperson named Bergliot Solberg a.k.a. The Cougar Lady, who became something of a legend as she stalked the streets of modern Sechelt in gumboots and cowboy hat, often toting a bale of hay and a couple jerry cans of kerosene. From time to time Sechelt tourism boosters attempt to promote the inlet as an "Inland Sea" packed with recreational wonders, but its appeal has always suffered in comparison with the more accessible cruising and better fishing on the outside. Still, for those who have already sampled the delights of Smuggler Cove, the Thormanbys, Pender Harbour, Hotham Sound and Jervis Inlet, Sechelt Inlet is a pleasant weekend cruising experience offering several pocket-sized marine parks, an unusual waterfall at Misery Creek that leaps out of a crack in

A torii gate at the entrance to Sechelt's waterfront pier stands in remembrance of Japanese residents who were interned in WWII.
Keith Thirkell

Right: Pacific white-sided dolphins in the waters near Sechelt. *Keith Thirkell*

Below: Sechelt Inlet's inside waters are great for kayaking. *Keith Thirkell*

the rock and spectacular wilderness hiking. For those who like scuba diving on artificial reefs, there is also the scuttled destroyer HMCS *Chaudiere* at the mouth of Salmon Inlet.

In Bert Whittaker's day it must have seemed that the inlet was going to play a much bigger role in the town's future. It was alive with large railway logging camps, there was a brick factory at Storm Bay, there were fishing resorts up Salmon Inlet, and the settlements at Doriston and Clowhom must have seemed as likely to develop into permanent communities as Egmont or Pender Harbour. Whittaker cornered the up-inlet trade by building the first wharves on both sides of the Sechelt isthmus, and for three decades the wagon path that connected them, still called Wharf Road, was the busiest street in town. New opportunities opened up for men like "French Pete" Levesque, a party-loving roustabout who felled a big fir tree, hacked off two approximately round slices to serve as wheels, attached them to a plank box, scrounged up a nag to pull it, and started the Peninsula's first overland freight hauling business. One day between deliveries French Pete retired to his shack and blew his brains out, an act only those of us who later tried to make a buck hauling stuff on Sunshine Coast roads can fully appreciate.

It was not until the mid-1950s, when the Sunshine Coast Highway was completed with ferries at both ends, that the Sechelt's east–west axis along Cowrie Street began to overshadow north–south traffic along Wharf, but either way Sechelt was going to capitalize. Situated on a crossroads at the geographical centre of the Baja Sunshine Coast, Sechelt was and is the strategic location for a regional trading hub, and Whittaker's descendants have carried on with his example. It was a cousin of Whittaker's, E.S. Clayton, who grandfathered the family which still operates the ever-expanding Trail Bay Mall and several other leading businesses in town.

Despite its significant location, Sechelt has for most of its history played second fiddle to Gibsons in terms of size and influence, although the balance began to shift through the 1980s and '90s as more and more region-wide services followed the example of St. Mary's Hospital (formerly located in Pender Harbour) and set up shop in the middle of things. By the mid-1990s the two areas were about the same size, at roughly 6,000 people each. This trend is viewed with alarm by Gibsons, which is reluctant to relinquish its position as big sister among

Above left: Wharf Road, joining Sechelt's two all-important steamboat docks, used to be Sechelt's main—and only—street.

Above: Bergliot Solberg, a.k.a "The Cougar Lady" (taking aim), was raised with her sister, Minnie, in the wilds of Sechelt Inlet. *Keith Thirkell*

Above: Sechelt's Festival of the Written Arts is known and copied across Canada.
Teresa Nightengale

Right: Sunshine Coasters are huge vintage car fans and Sechelt puts on a great show and shine every year.

Coasters are mad gardeners.
Allan Forest

Previous pages: Mountain-girt Phantom Lake, a challenging hike inland from the head of Salmon Inlet, is one of the coast's scenic treasures. It has recently been impacted by a private hydro project.

Baja towns and is loath to concede any advantages to its upcoast underlings for any cause. This leads to a standoff when it comes to such issues as pooling resources to build a recreation complex for the coast, which neither town can afford on its own but neither can bring itself to support unless the concrete gets poured within its own bailiwick. The result is a generally low level of services considering the combined tax base of the whole area, and duplication of what little there is. It has become quite popular for tub-thumpers of various stripes to decry the situation and call for a general union of all coastal communities from Egmont to Dogpatch, but until some Solomon solves the riddle of who will get the centralized infrastructure, the plan is likely to remain in the municipality of conjecture. For my part, I am just as happy. I believe our distinctive communities are a precious resource, and the longer the Sunshine Coast can avoid mushing together into one big faceless Surrey North, the better.

A certain noxious crank, reflecting on Sechelt's mercantile proclivities, once called it "a seaside shopping town that hasn't progressed an intellectual hair's breadth since Sinclair Lewis put the North American shopping town under glass in *Babbitt*." While it may be argued the Chamber of Commerce and Rotary Club play a more prominent role in Sechelt affairs than is perhaps advisable or safe, no town that calls its main drag Teredo Street can be all bad.

Indeed, modern Sechelt is a village of several dimensions. It boasts not one but two busy arts centres: Rockwood Lodge, a handsomely restored heritage building punctuating the western end of Cowrie Street, and the Sunshine Coast Arts Centre, located in an unusual high-tech log cabin on Trail Avenue. The town has been for some years home of the Sechelt Festival of the Written Arts, an outstanding literary festival that has attracted the likes of Margaret Atwood, Alice Munro and Al Purdy. Sechelt is also the home turf of the Sechelt Indian Band, one of the most progressive First Nations in Canada.

IF RECENT IMMIGRANTS TO THE SUNSHINE Coast have demonstrated a tendency to follow their own drummer, they appear to be continuing a trend well established by the area's first inhabitants. Before the arrival of European explorers in the late 1700s, the Sunshine Coast had been shared since the last ice age by three different aboriginal groups, the Squamish (Howe Sound), the Sechelt (Sechelt Peninsula), and the Sliammon (Powell River). By all accounts they were exceptional peoples.

Although the Sunshine Coast nations considered themselves independent, anthropologists group them together in a linguistic and cultural family known as Coast Salish. They enjoyed a comparatively comfortable existence owing to their benign climate and an abundance of easily obtained food, principally salmon, herring, venison and berries. The Coast Salish have never enjoyed the renown accorded by white Native-fanciers to the Haida and Kwakiutl, probably because the Salish didn't erect forests of totem poles, didn't carve sea-going war canoes, and didn't produce world-class art—except on one notable occasion. On the other hand, they didn't use the bodies of freshly killed slaves for boat ramps. What they did do was create a social order that came closer to that of modern democracies in terms of respect for human life and individual freedom. Among the Northern tribes, only those born to noble families could hope to achieve high standing through membership in secret cannibal and dog-eating societies, but every member of a Salish tribe had the opportunity to seek his or her individual *sulia* or power through a spirit quest that was open to all comers, and leadership was based on

Bald eagles still know where to find the fish.

merit as much as on inherited privilege. There was no single, all-powerful chief, but a collective of male and female leaders all honoured with the same respectful term, in sháshishálhem (Sechelt) language *hiwus*.

In their heyday, the Sechelt occupied the bulk of the territory now known as the Sunshine Coast with some eighty villages. So numerous were the lodge fires of the Sechelt nation, elders used to speak of a time when there was "one big smoke" from Gower Point to Saltery Bay. The main tribal groupings were centred around four principal villages at Hunaechin (at the head of Jervis Inlet), Tsonai (at Deserted Bay, Jervis Inlet), Tuwanek (in Sechelt Inlet) and Kalpalin (Pender Harbour).

(Under the direction of Dr. Ronald Beaumont of the University of BC, the Sechelt have standardized Sechelt spellings using a specialized orthography, but because I don't have space to explain how the orthography works, I will eschew it for the more familiar of the anglicized usages and write "Sechelt" instead of "shíshálh.")

Unlike some Coast Salish tribes, who stayed put in their ancestral villages year-round, the Sechelt congregated for the winter ceremonials in one composite mega-village at Kalpalin on the shores of Pender Harbour. Although some band publications place their original population at 20,000, scholarly estimates range between 5,000 and 8,000.

The undoing of this great Native nation began early on. The Roman Catholic missionary Father Leon Fouquet of the Oblate Order visited Kalpalin in 1860, urging all to abandon the beliefs of their ancestors and accept the god of the white man. Not surprisingly, Fouquet was sent packing. But only two years later, the Sechelt invited the Oblates back and submitted to a rigorous Christian regime under Father (later Bishop) Paul Durieu. Some writers present this simply as a case of children of darkness seeing the light, but there was more to it. Earlier in 1862 the worst smallpox epidemic in BC history swept like a tsunami through the coast's Native communities. How many Sechelt died isn't known, but an unofficial head count several years later found them reduced to less than one-tenth of their peak numbers, and much of this decrease must have occurred in 1862. Clearly, the Sechelt people who turned back to the missionaries in the aftermath of the plague were not the same people who had so confidently rejected them two years earlier. With their own medicine men exposed as powerless against the menace of the white man's diseases, their leadership in shambles and the great family groups reduced to a few bewildered survivors, their appeal to the church was less a reasoned choice than an act of desperation.

It may also have been an act of fear. Major illness was understood by aboriginal peoples of the coast to be caused by hostile forces in the spirit world. The immediate source of trouble was typically thought to be a hostile medicine man, who would either have to be overcome or placated, depending on how powerful he was. When the early missionaries told Native people the devastating epidemics were God's punishment for refusing His Word, it was all too plausible in terms of their traditional belief. The awesome force of the diseases suggested

Artist Gaye Hammond's conception of Sawquamain, winter headquarters of the 5,000-strong Sechelt Nation at Garden Bay in Pender Harbour prior to 1862. Coast Salish longhouses were enormous; Simon Fraser measured one 800 feet long near Chilliwack.

Opposite top left: Mushroom collecting is a popular fall pastime in Sunshine Coast hills. Pine mushrooms are especially sought-after.

Opposite top right: The red huckleberry, a much appreciated rainforest shrub.

Opposite bottom: Tetrahedron Provincial Park protects the headwaters of the Chapman and Gray Creek watersheds—the water supply of the Sunshine Coast. *Keith Thirkell*

these new black-robed medicine men were too powerful to be resisted and had to be placated for the good of the tribe. It is no coincidence that the two greatest mass conversions in northwest coast history—by William Duncan among the Tsimshian and Durieu among the Sechelt—both occurred in the days immediately following the smallpox epidemic. With its terrifying example to back up his persuasions, Durieu was able to administer the sacrament of confirmation to every last man, woman and child in the Sechelt nation.

Like Duncan, Durieu followed the popular colonial practice of removing converts from their ancestral grounds and gathering them together on a new site where the church could reign supreme. The site he selected was one Sechelt tribes had occupied only sporadically over the centuries because it was exposed to weather and attack, it lacked adequate drinking water and generally didn't have much to recommend it from an aboriginal point of view. This was the site of modern-day Sechelt. Over the next three decades the Oblates forged a Christian community at Sechelt, which became the showpiece of "the Durieu System," a theocratic regime featuring police-state discipline and rigorous suppression of aboriginal culture, later copied at Oblate missions among the Sliammon, Squamish and others.

Durieu was a strict puritan who didn't allow his own French and Belgian priests to drink wine in private and in one oft-repeated anecdote broke up Sechelt preparations for a soccer tournament with the Nanaimos, confiscated the ball and ordered players and spectators alike to get to work ditching a swamp. In another story he prevailed upon some Sliammon men to paddle him down to Sechelt, a trip of some seventy miles. Midway they stopped for lunch. On previous occasions the arrangement had been that the priest would supply food for the men who gave their time to paddle him, but on this occasion Durieu was miffed because the band was resisting church pressure for increased cash contributions. He broke out a large basket and feasted himself ostentatiously before the hungry men. When one of them asked where their food was, Durieu said, "Eat wood, it is good enough for disobedient boys as you are." They had to carry the priest the rest of the way to Sechelt on empty stomachs. When Bishop E.M. Bunoz passed the same way fifteen years later, they were still talking about it.

Durieu espoused the belief that "Indians are only big children" and governed accordingly. The whole village was compelled to rise each morning at the first bell and attend church for prayers. An evening bell called them for a second daily round of prayers. Shortly after, a curfew bell was the signal for all lights to be put out. The punishment for missing church was the same as for adultery: forty lashes. On one occasion the flogging got so far out of hand one of Durieu's lieutenants, Father Chirouse, was convicted and jailed by civil court.

Native culture was strictly suppressed. As Bishop Bunoz wrote in a warm appreciation of his predecessor's system in 1941:

> Our Indians had to give up all of their old fashioned amusements because they contained some traces of paganism and superstition. So they made bonfires with their century-old totem poles. They had to burn rattles, expensive coats and other paraphernalia of the medicine men...Potlatches great and small were forbidden. Gambling, dancing and some winter festivities had to be abandoned. Bishop Durieu strictly exacted the abolition of the above practices because they were opposed to pure Christianity, but he knew well that the Indians had to have some amusements and that the pagan feasts had to be replaced by Christian ones.

Under Durieu's direction the Sechelt made a name for themselves by building a European-style townsite, touring a brass band and theatre troupe that staged elaborate passion plays around BC, and by diligently applying themselves to such non-traditional economic pursuits as logging, commercial fishing and commercial hunting for the fresh meat trade in Vancouver.

Viewing the results of Durieu's cultural makeover of the Sechelt three decades after it began, ethnologist Charles Hill-Tout reported:

> Of all the native races of this province, they are probably the most modified by white influences. They are now, outwardly at least, a civilized people, and their lives compare favourably with the better class of peasants of Western Europe. Their permanent tribal home, or headquarters, contains about a hundred well-built cottages, many of them two-storied, and some of them having as many as six rooms. Each house has its own garden plot attached to it in which are grown European fruits and vegetables. In the centre of the whole stands an imposing church, which cost the tribe nearly $8,000 a few years ago. Nearby, they have a commodious and well-built meeting room, or public hall, capable of holding 500 persons or more, and a handsome pavilion or band-stand fronts the bay. They possess also a convenient and effective waterworks system of their own...every street has its hydrants at intervals of forty or fifty yards. As a body, the Sechelt are, without doubt, the most industrious and prosperous of all the Native peoples of this province...they owe their tribal and individual prosperity mainly, if not entirely, to the Fathers of the Oblate Mission.

Twelve totem poles look out over Trail Bay in Sechelt and depict the history of the Sechelt Nation.

IN FACT THE SECHELT HAD NOT FLOURISHED in the care of the church. Population had continued to decline at an alarming rate until by the time of the first official census in 1881, there were only 167 survivors left from the original body of over 5,000. The prim little community Hill-Tout viewed so approvingly in 1902 was but a sad remnant of the sprawling aboriginal nation that had united all the inlets and islands of the Sunshine Coast in "one smoke" a hundred years earlier. In the century since, the Sechelt have recovered steadily but slowly. By 2006 official band membership numbered over 1,200, 600 of whom lived away from band lands. Most of the fabulous repertoire of songs and dances and ceremonial art that had enlivened the great festival season at Kalpalin was lost, but some were acquired by neighbouring tribes on Vancouver Island who still perform with them today.

One outstanding artifact remaining from pre-historic times is the "Sechelt Image," a twenty-inch-tall granite statuette discovered under a tree root by boys playing at Selma Park in 1921. I am informed that Sechelt elders of today view the figure as a mother holding her child *only*—with the emphasis on "only" because other observers, like the late anthropologist Wilson Duff, described it as "the very image of masculine strength, stated in the metaphor of sex. His head is powerfully masculine, and he clasps a huge phallus; the whole boulder, seen backwards and upside down, is phallic in form."

I stopped by the gallery just before writing this to check it over once more, and I'm afraid

Above: Master carver Arnold Jones works on a memorial totem pole on site at the Egmont Heritage Centre. *Allan Forest*

Right: Sechelt Band member Lakota Joe hoists the Olympic torch. *Allan Forest*

Above and left: Participants in workshops at the Téms Swíya Museum. *Allan Forest*

75

I have to side with Duff. For me, all doubt about the sexual connotations of the work is resolved by taking the posterior view, which slyly transforms the whole sculpture into a massive phallus, replete with bulging veins. Not to be overlooked is the anterior view, which reveals a prominent vulva.

Was some antique wit trying to sum up the entire sexual experience of humankind at one go? The way images of raging sexuality and serene parenthood are coupled in one ambiguous whole startles the viewer with its modernness, reaching across the erosion of the centuries with a cheeky freshness. No wonder Duff pronounced the Sechelt Image "a great work of stone sculpture" and the director of the Victoria Art Gallery, Richard Simmins, was inspired to make it the centrepiece of "Images: Stone: B.C.," a seminal exhibition of Northwest Coast Indian stone sculpture that toured Canada in 1975. This enigmatic, powerful masterwork, along with some good examples of Sechelt weaving and carving, can be viewed in the band's Téms Swíya Museum in Sechelt.

Today's Sechelt feel sadly cut off from the traditions of their aboriginal past, and they carry on few ceremonial activities compared to the neighbouring Cowichan and Squamish. They pursue a vigorous language preservation project with the help of Dr. Beaumont and several families and have revived the practice of giving potlatches (tl'e?enaks) to bestow traditional names, which they research in old church records. The late Mary Craigan had tears in her eyes as she recounted to me her experience attending a Cowichan ceremony where she witnessed some of the ancient songs and dances that were once performed by her ancestors at Kalpalin. It was the first time she had heard them but they had worked a powerful spell over her she had no words to describe, as if pulling at something deep inside. Granny Craigan struggled alongside other elders to excavate memories of their people's past to fulfill younger members' reawakening thirst for tribal identity, but it is hard digging. Native or non, who could say what their ancestors did and thought over a century ago, especially when the main written record has been kept by people dedicated to erasing the heritage?

Something that has survived intact is the Sechelt's talent for commerce. They have been involved in the operation of an offshore trawler, a local airline, a salmon hatchery, an office and cultural complex, a large gravel-mining project, a McDonald's restaurant franchise and other business enterprises.

But it is in the political arena that the Sechelt have most distinguished themselves. From the earliest times when Chief Tom Tsohnye made land claims representations to Victoria, through the activism of such leaders as Caspar John, Joe La Dally, Dan Paull, Reg Paull, Charlie Craigan, Henry Paull, Stan Dixon and Clarence Joe—a consummate statesman who addressed both the Canadian House of Commons and the United Nations—the Sechelt charted their own course through Canadian politics, far in advance of most other First Nations groups.

Their first goal was to free themselves from the shackles of the Canadian Indian Act, which deprived them of the full rights of citizenship and greatly restricted their mercantile inclinations. After a long campaign by a succession of Sechelt leaders, the federal parliament passed Bill C-93, The Sechelt Indian Band Self-Government Act of 1986, making them the first band in Canada to achieve native self-government. This proved controversial within the community of First Nations, since the Sechelt had taken a very pragmatic view of self-government, one characterized by the Grand Council of Crees as "identical to the model of the municipalities." This is not quite true since the Sechelt have extra-municipal powers over education, social services, health and public order, and Section 38 of the Self-Government Act declares that the "constitution of the Band or the law of the Band" can take precedence over the laws of BC.

The Sechelt Image is a masterwork of aboriginal stone sculpture on view at the band museum in Sechelt. *Allan Forest*

76

Other bands held out for something closer to full provincial status and denounced the Sechelt solution as a sellout. The Sechelt leaders of the day viewed the grander claims as unrealizable, and held that gains negotiated under their self government agreements were underestimated by their critics.

Since 1986 more bands across Canada have been taking a second look at the Sechelt model, and the Nishga'a settlement of 1996 owes something to it, but for the most part the Sechelt remain defiantly out of step with their brethren on the national stage. For the original oddball residents of the Sunshine Coast, that is perhaps just as it should be.

AN EXCELLENT WAY TO PAUSE AND REFLECT upon one's visit to Sechelt used to be by taking an ale and chowder on the sundeck of the Wakefield Inn, but since that historic old log lodge overlooking the beach at Wakefield Creek in West Sechelt has been replaced by condos, the Lighthouse Pub at Porpoise Bay is a good substitute. Though not so restful as the old Wakefield, it has a generous deck built right over the water and you can spend many an entertaining hour there enjoying the comings and goings of float planes, work boats and pleasure craft bound to and from the upper reaches of Sechelt Inlet. It is my favourite place

The Lighthouse Pub overlooks the busy Porpoise Bay waterfront.

to go on a sunny summer day—along with the decks at the Garden Bay Hotel in Pender Harbour and the Backeddy in Egmont. It has always puzzled me why there are so few eating and drinking places on the coast that recognize the one best attraction they could offer patrons is something the coast has in cheap abundance—a good view of the ocean, with outdoor tables in season. You'd think there would be dozens, but there aren't. This may reflect the values of local patrons. Inside the Lighthouse or the Backeddy you may be lucky enough to spot authentic examples of these, easily distinguishable by their traditional Sunshine Coast dress—battered baseball caps, red suspenders, grey Stanfields underwear tops serving as outerwear—a fashion known locally as the "Texada tuxedo"—and elastic-sided boots known as "fishermen's slippers." You can also detect true locals by their placement in the pub—away from the windows with their back to the view. This isn't to say their talk is any less concerned with solving the mysteries of the universe. It's just that they've got the view memorized.

JUST NORTH OF WAKEFIELD BEACH—THE HIGHWAY IS actually running west at this stage, but locals think of it as north—the route up the Peninsula divides between the new highway and the old highway, now called Redrooffs Road. Redrooffs Road snakes along the waterfront for about five miles to the tiny village of Halfmoon Bay and doesn't actually provide many open views, but it does let on to some fine places to get down to the sea. The first of these is at Sargeant Bay, where local government has created a small park featuring a wildfowl marsh and a very pretty pebble beach. Another worthwhile stop comes up a few miles farther

Trout Lake's convenient location beside the highway at Halfmoon Bay makes it a popular recreation area.

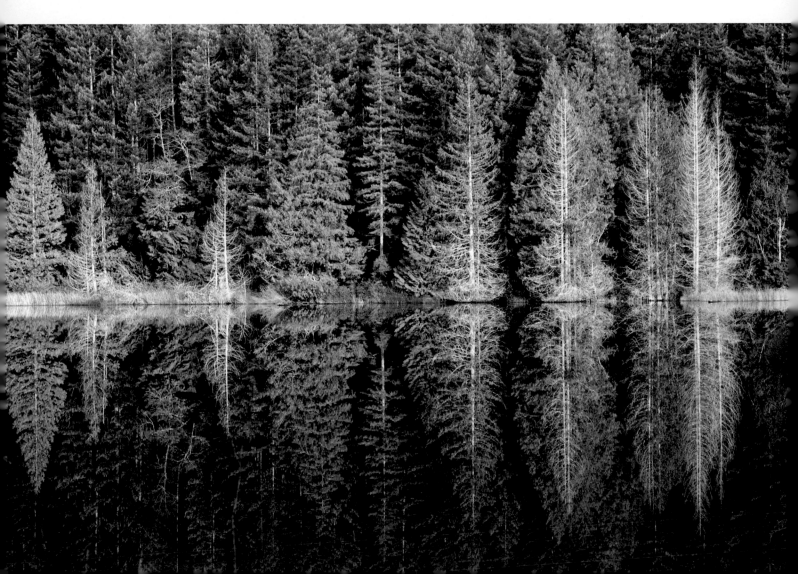

Most of the coast's communities are served by volunteer fire departments. *Allan Forest*

Above: The Halfmoon Bay Store has changed little since the days when steamships called at the nearby wharf.

Left: Sargeant Bay Park features a pretty pebble beach and marsh.

Left: Shoreline near
Smuggler Cove on
a windy day.

Below: Boats anchored at
Buccaneer Bay, Thormanby
Island, a popular beach area.

Opposite: Secret Cove is
a beguiling complex of islets
and passages.

Above: The Thormanby Islands, great for every kind of marine recreation.

Above right: Scenic shoreline in Simson Marine Park, South Thormanby Island.

along, where a steep lane lets down to Welcome Beach. The name has an ironic tinge, for while the antique summer cabins that crowd the seafront esplanade are picturesque and the beach itself is very welcoming, the inhabitants of this cozy corner of paradise have a way of making non-residents feel as welcome as skunks at a garden party. You can reassure yourself that nobody owns the beach and brazen out the stares, or retreat to the regional park a few minutes' drive up the road at Cooper's Green. This also has a gravel wading beach along the eastern shore of Halfmoon Bay, and makes a good base for one of the most remarkable days of micro-cruising or gunkholing it is possible to take.

The Halfmoon Bay–Secret Cove area is probably the nearest thing to a saltwater labyrinth one is likely to find this side of Homer's Aegean. The sea-flooded stone formations here are as intricate as the folds of Einstein's brain, and the average brain can become thoroughly befuddled trying to keep track of which filament-like passageway, which hidden lagoon or which miniature islet is which. Smuggler Cove Marine Park is the most famous example of this "drowned landscape," but Frenchman's Cove on the west shore of Halfmoon Bay is equally fine. Secret Cove just up the shore offers more of the same on a somewhat coarser scale, heavily overlaid with condos and marinas. The area truly offers one of the most mesmerizing boating experiences on the coast, but it is all in miniature. A sea kayak would be a good vehicle for exploring it, and Cooper's Green offers good launching for car toppers or runabouts. The smaller the boat the more of the area's impossible intricacy you can probe. Just up the shore at Ole's Cove, Rockwater Resort offers one of the more reliable menus on the coast—and a sea view.

82

Across Welcome Pass, joining North and South Thormanby islands is Buccaneer Bay, a low sandy spit with the sweetest swimming and sunning beach south of Savary Island. South Thormanby was preempted at the turn of the twentieth century by a sober British ironmonger named Calvert Simson, who at the time was storekeeper of the Hastings Mill Store in the town of Granville before it became Vancouver. He built a summer home beside the spit, cleared a farm down at the south end and lavished the island with fussy care for half a century before turning it over to his son, George Joe, who carried on in the same manner until 1975 when he persuaded a reluctant provincial government to accept it as a free gift to the people of BC. Simson Marine Park is larger than Vancouver's Stanley Park or New York's Central Park, and after paddling through the seal rookery at Bertha Rock, poking your nose into the enchanted granite grottos on the south end and picnicking at the old farm, you will probably agree it's more attractive than either. It's sobering to think we almost didn't get it because the conservative politicians of the day didn't want to forgo a few dollars' worth of private land taxes.

Provided the log tugs are still indicating fair weather, a good way to top off the day's paddling is to pay a visit to the Sunshine Coast's only lighthouse, on Merry Island just a cattywampus across the chuck from Simson Park. As late as 2011 it was still a manned station, but federal bureaucrats in faraway Ottawa were waging a relentless campaign to replace the keepers with automated gadgetry that would ultimately be more expensive to maintain, would not provide the tugs with weather reports they could trust, and would not dash out to save you should your kayak be surprised by a westerly squall. It's the kind of thing that keeps debate on the merits of confederation a live issue on the West Coast.

Merry Island, the Sunshine Coast's only staffed lighthouse, guards the entrance to Welcome Pass.

PENDER HARBOUR DUPLICATES the drowned landscape complexity of the coves on a yet larger scale. The main harbour is only a mile and a half in length, but taking all the wrinkles into account, it has 103 miles of total shoreline. The whole performance involves three coves, six lagoons, twenty bays, twenty-nine reefs, thirty-one islands, one tidal narrows, one drying pass, two reversing saltwater waterfalls and Whiskey Slough. It takes ninety seconds to go from Pope Landing to Irvines Landing on the other side of the harbour in a slow kicker boat, or half an hour to drive by fast car, which is why for the first half-century Pender people did everything by boat—shop, visit, go to school, go to church. With dozens of little kickers crisscrossing the lagoons and bays at all times of the day and night, and a dock in front of every home, the comparison to Venice was obvious, but nowadays most people find it somehow more convenient to make the half-hour drive. The community is still laid out around the harbour, however, and it is only when toured by water it really makes sense. Negotiating the twists and turns by auto, it can take years before new residents can honestly say they know just where they are at any given time, and few long-term Harbourites could draw the place accurately without checking a map.

Such crenellated geography has worked its influence on the nature of the community. In aboriginal times the villages were separated from each other, as if compartmentalized by the landscape. People in the main village of Sawquamain in Garden Bay had limited contact with

Pender Harbour boasts the finest natural harbour on the Sunshine Coast.

those at the Sallahlus village in Madeira Park, whom they considered without status. Present-day Garden Bay residents have at times been suspected of feeling the same way about Madeira Parkers, and vice versa. When I first came to the Harbour in 1950, its small population was partitioned into resolutely separate communities at Irvines Landing, Pope Landing, Donley Landing, Garden Bay, Kleindale and Madeira Park. Each place had its own school, store and community hall and tried to have as little as possible to do with the others. Turf wars over such matters as where to locate a new high school or credit union office were savage. Life was complicated further by a social structure based on big families, each firmly rooted in its own territory. The Lees held sway at Irvines, the Reids in Garden Bay, the Kleins at Kleindale, the Warnocks in Bargain Harbour, the Camerons and MacKays in Whiskey Slough. Before the Second World War, when they were interned on two hours' notice, there had been another quite separate group made up of Japanese families—the Ikedas, Kawasakis and Okasas. When the Anglican minister Rev. Alan Greene of the Columbia Coast Mission began trying to organize Harbourites to construct the central Sunshine Coast hospital at Garden Bay in the late 1920s, he had the damnedest time trying to get people to put aside their native animosities,

Pender Harbour has long been home port to a commercial fishing fleet.
Keith Thirkell

Above: Pender Harbour's May Day celebration has been running for over half a century—and always brings out the sun. *Allan Forest*

Above right: Pender Harbour is the world epicentre of longboard racing, thanks to former local Bricin Lyons. *Allan Forest*

Right: In Pender Harbour's April Tools race, contestants must first build their boats then paddle them to the finish. *Allan Forest*

and his daughter Barbara told me he was bedevilled by the community's irascible nature all the years he ran the hospital.

The poet Patrick Lane, a sometime Middle Point resident who moved back to the coast in the 1990s after living fifteen years on the prairies, remarked that the people of the coast in general were strikingly in-turned compared to the prairie types, who are much more open and sociable. The difference was so marked and so general he couldn't help thinking the wide-open geography of the prairie and the closed, compartmentalized geography of the coast were somehow reflected in the personalities of the people. In this sense Pender Harbour is like the coast in general, just a little more so.

IT'S HARD TO CONTEMPLATE THE CENTURY OF non-Native history of Pender Harbour without being aware how insignificant it is beside the aboriginal history of the place. Although it is well established that the Harbour was the winter home of the Sechelt Nation and one of the larger Native communities on the West Coast, very little has been written on it and no serious study has been made of the area's very rich archaeological history. The anthropologist Homer Barnett, who visited Pender Harbour in 1935, mentions only the main settlement at Sawquamain in Garden Bay and one other to the south—presumably Sallahlus at Bargain Narrows. My own experience from a lifetime of excavating around Pender Harbour—not as an archaeologist, but as an interested ditch digger—is that there must have been almost continuous settlement around the entire 103 miles of harbour shoreline. I once had a job installing a sewer system on the Sallahlus reserve and found myself digging down in ancient fire ash and clamshell deposits to a depth of six feet, encountering not a few human skulls along

The May Queen and Princesses pass by the Madeira Park community hall during the annual May Day parade. *Allan Forest*

Above: Shellfish were a staple of the Sechelt First Nation's diet.

Right and opposite: Rock paintings, like those at Sakinaw lake (opposite), are found across the Sunshine Coast and are a link to the aboriginal past. *Keith Thirkell*

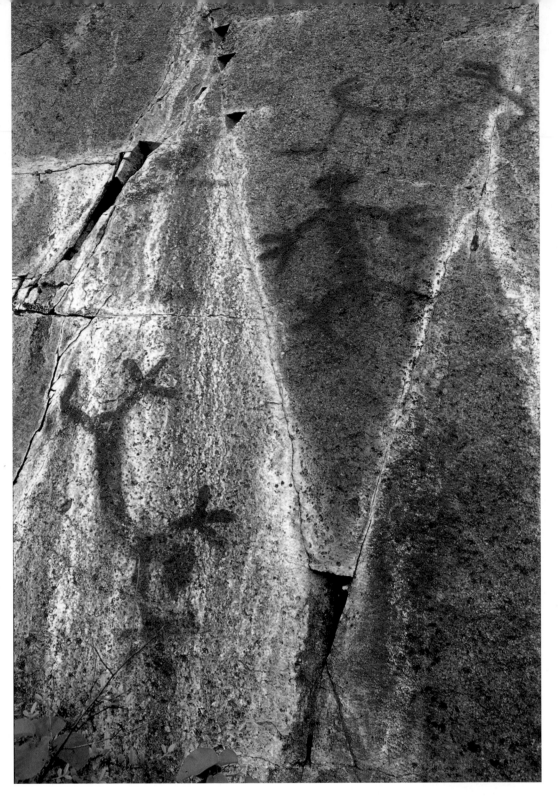

the way. There was another large deposit of bone-laden midden soil at Irvines Landing at the mouth of the Harbour, and sizable ones at Gerrans Bay and on the fertile mudflats at the head of Oyster Bay, a site known as Smeshalin. When my father and I were excavating basements around Pender Harbour in the 1960s I became accustomed to rooting up cooking rocks and clamshell anywhere there was a pocket of dirt big enough to sink a muckstick into. Many sites were chock-full of human remains, sad evidence of the fate that befell these historic villages.

The Sechelt traditionally left their dead above ground on special burial islands like the two unnamed islets at the north end of Bargain Narrows. My school mate Ab Haddock and I lived

90

The spectacular arbutus tree flourishes all along the Sunshine Coast.

on opposite sides of Gerrans Bay a stone's throw from those islets, and he used to make me jealous with all the nifty artifacts he dug up on them, but the rest of us kids lacked the nerve to disturb them. We were afraid of awakening smoldering embers of the last smallpox epidemic, which to us seemed still to lurk very near at hand, although it had died out a century earlier. It was easy to see that such a tiny burial ground would have been inadequate during the great plague of 1862, when the people fell in such numbers survivors were forced to convert many of the prime village sites into mass graves. More burying took place after the Sechelt's conversion to Catholicism, when the priests ordered that remains that had been set out in the traditional way be gathered up and placed underground in the European manner. There were dozens of bone-filled midden sites around the shores of Pender Harbour, many of them sizable, and most uncatalogued. Since it takes many years to build up an inch of permanent midden soil, these heavy deposits bear witness to the immense scale and intensity of the living that must have taken place here before the Europeans arrived with their deadly diseases. It's

92

enough to make the late Gilbert Joe's estimate of 20,000 residents seem plausible, but even if the lowest estimate of 5,000 is correct, it would have made Kalpalin more densely populated in 1800 than Pender Harbour was in 2011—and that was just counting local residents. During big feasts, potlatches, or trading days, that number would be swelled by other Salish groups visiting from neighbouring areas.

Viewing the modest mostly-white village of 2,500 reposing on the shores of the landlocked harbour basin today, it's hard to picture the same scene rocking under the sway of ten or twenty thousand celebrants, but if you'd dropped in between October and March a few brief centuries ago, that may well be what you'd have seen.

The Salish had an admirable grasp of what really mattered in life. They were tremendous workers and they laboured mightily all summer putting up dried salmon and making salal berry leather as well as dozens of other labour-intensive tasks involved in maintaining well-run stone-age households, like weaving watertight baskets of spruce root and washing used ones with a putrefied fungus known as *xwat'Kimunach* or "thunder shit." Everyday dress consisted of aprons made of deer hide or woven from cedar bark. Cedar bark was also woven into blankets and robes, as was wool from mountain goat and special long-haired dogs. Twine for fishing line and nets was woven from nettle fibre. Plentiful stands of red cedar provided easily worked building materials for dugout canoes, feast bowls and plank-walled dwellings, some of which were enormous. According to pioneer ethnologist Charles Hill-Tout, who studied the Sechelt in the summer of 1902, Sechelt houses had "a platform about two feet high and five or six feet broad erected all around the inside walls. This served as seats or lounges for the occupants during the day, and during the night as beds. Some ten or twelve feet above this platform small isolated cubicles or sleeping rooms were constructed...Each family partitioned off its allotment from the rest by means of hanging mats."

Abstract designs in yellow cedar.

The work of the Salish summer was performed with the aim of freeing the winter for social activities. Anthropologists are fond of referring to the winter activities of the Salish as "ceremonials," which they depict as some kind of joyless neolithic ritual. My old Squamish friend Dominic Charlie, who kept performing his sensational leaping deer dance until he was in his eighties, remembered it differently. "In them old times," Dominic told me, "we just dance and dance all winter long. Just dance and dance. Everybody he go to that big house and dance all night long and all day long. All winter he keep doing that. Oh, we had great times in them old times."

Great times. That's what the Salish winter was all about. Most people had their own special dance that had come to them in a dream or vision accompanied by a song, and often gave them a special power associated with an animal. One renowned hunter imitated killer whales in his dance. He had got this dance one night when he approached a beach where people were dancing around a campfire, but turned into killer whales and swam away when he got close. In the dream that followed he got not only the dance and a song, but the killer whale's power to hunt seals, sea lions and porpoises. Another prominent man had the wolf dance, which he got when he fell and wounded his leg while stripping bark from a tree. When he awoke a wolf was licking his wound. In his dream he received a song featuring the cry of the wolf and a dance in which he ate the flesh of live dogs. Men's dances tended to be associated with major animals like the bear and mountain goat, while women were often left with lesser spirits like the duck, crane, quail and even the blowfly.

In addition to dancing, there were events of more distinctly spiritual nature such as initiation rites for young dancers taking possession of their own special dances and performances by medicine men. Sechelt shamans were particularly noted for their miraculous performances. The Tsonai leader Joe La Dally told anthropologist Homer Barnett of an occasion when a shaman named Kaltopa was called to attend a dying man. He brought with him the skins of seven different animals—otter, mink, raccoon, fox, loon, eagle and marten. After singing his spirit song, he blew on each skin and it came to life, scampering around on the floor uttering its natural cry. He then covered his head with a blanket and began to grope on the floor in search of the patient's missing soul. His own spirit was thought to have departed from his body at this point because at length he uttered a *whoo-ing* noise as if returning from a great distance. Finally the shaman rose, holding the retrieved soul in his hands. When it was returned to its rightful place the patient showed immediate signs of recovery, and his brother asked the shaman if he knew who'd taken the errant soul. The shaman said that he indeed did, whereupon the brother requested the evildoer be put to death. The shaman again covered his head and began groping on the floor. After

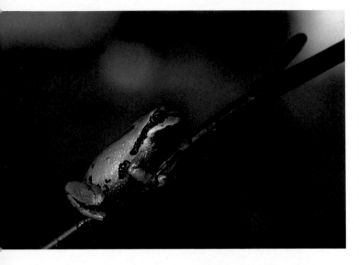

The Pacific tree frog changes colour with amazing rapidity.

about half an hour the sounds of the returning spirit were heard once more, and the shaman leapt to his feet to reveal in the palm of his hand a tiny human body. He held the miniature form over the fire and squeezed it until blood ran out between his fingers, then dropped the small shape into the flames. At that moment a well-known Comox shaman keeled over stone dead, according to a Sechelt villager who had been visiting in Comox.

His duties completed, Kaltopa deflated his skins, packed up and left. The purpose of the skins had been to watch over the patient while the medicine man was out of his body stalking his foe in the spirit realm.

Barnett was able to obtain a corroborating version of this story from another Sechelt elder, Charlie Roberts, who added that Kaltopa's return was assisted by other Sechelt shamans who guided him back with choruses of their own *whoo-ing* in answer to his. Roberts added that he'd seen another shaman who could perform the miracle of bringing animal skins to life, and in addition possessed a big quartz crystal he could activate to dance and whirl around on the floor with a whining sound. Shamanic performances of this kind were a regular and popular feature of winter dances, along with feasting and potlatching, the ceremonial giving of property to enhance status. There were also lively trading extravaganzas, especially among the Sechelt, who have always been among the coast's great wheeler-dealers.

Kalpalin's principal settlement at Sawquamain, in the area now known as Garden Bay, was crowded with seven huge longhouses, four ranked one behind the other while the other three ran crosswise farther inland. Each had an attached woodshed and a spacious outdoor platform suitable for staging potlatches, an architectural feature my friend Gilbert Joe referred to as "the Sunshine Coast's first sundecks." Like modern-day homes on the Sunshine Coast, which announce themselves to passing traffic as "Taki-Teasy" or "Dunworkin" (my favourite is "Sechelter"), each of the Sawquamain lodges had its own name. There was "Right on the

The western red cedar prefers moist ground.

Beach," "Back Side House" and "Down in the Hole." The largest house Lester Peterson records as "The Kluh-uhn'-ahk-ahwt" (tlʼeʼlenakawt, or potlatch house), used only when the far-flung villagers were gathered together for communal events. There were no totem poles but "Right on the Beach" had a sea lion head carved onto the end of the ridgepole and the fifth lodge had posts topped with carvings of eagles. Salish houses weren't as finely crafted as those of the northern tribes, but they were bigger. Simon Fraser observed one near Chilliwack which was 800 feet long and 300 feet wide, and Charlie Roberts told Hill-Tout the greatest of the lodges at Sawquamain towered fifty feet in height.

NOT ALL OF THE SECHELT'S TROUBLES BEGAN with the arrival of the white man, of course. The main problem was their vulnerability to attack by other First Nations, a vulnerability increased by their wealth and their nonviolent nature. The word "schʼekʼlt" or "fort" occurs frequently in Sechelt place names, and according to Peterson a real fort replete with wooden palisade and moat stood near the head of Jervis Inlet until historic times. Another fort existed on Thormanby Island, where the exposed Sxwelap village made frequent use of it to fend off sea-going marauders from Kwakwa̱kaʼwakw territory. My old school chum Ron

95

The best way to make sense of Pender Harbour's tangled geography is by looking down on it from atop Mount Daniel. *Keith Thirkell*

Remmem, whose family home in Pender Harbour was close to the Sechelt's long-vanished winter capital of Sawquamain, used to talk about finding what looked like an ancient fort site on the slopes of nearby Mount Daniel. This matches stories Peterson collected of a fort on Mount Daniel that was used to shelter women and children during raids on Sawquamain. Barnett reports the big houses of Sawquamain had "subterranean retreats ready for use in case of surprise attacks...entered by tunnels leading from hidden openings inside." The late Clarence Joe used to tell me his people also kept sentries posted on Mount Daniel—and at many other places including Cape Cockburn to the north and Spyglass Hill to the south—to provide early warning of any suspicious traffic in surrounding waters.

Most raids were small affairs done by piratical rovers who picked off small groups of women and elders left unprotected during fishing or hunting forays, but large-scale massacres were not unknown. Peterson mentions a grassy flat east of Cockburn Bay on Nelson Island that got its name, *Swalth*, "from the fact that much blood was spilt there." He also used to tell me that the rocky knoll next to the property I grew up on at Madeira Park "was forever cursed by a powerful medicine man because of the slaughter suffered there by his people at the hands of early nineteenth-century raiders."

BY THE TIME I FIRST SAW PENDER HARBOUR IN 1950, only a few traces remained of the teeming, robust Salish city that made the Sechelt one of the great powers in the Northwest Coast Indian world. At Sakinaw Bay you could still trace among the barnacled beach rocks vague outlines of the elaborate stone fish trap that Professor Hill-Tout had described as a masterpiece of stone-age engineering a half-century earlier. Not long after, loggers perched an A-frame on the nearby bluff to skid logs out of Sakinaw Lake and promptly obliterated all trace of the ancient wonder. Atop Mount Daniel you could still trace outlines of the stone circles that were placed by girls during puberty rituals. In 1950 the aged chief Dan Johnson and his wife lived in a tumbledown shack that was all that remained of Sawquamain with its seven enormous longhouses. Eugene Paul lived on a landlocked scrap of land in Gerrans Bay and the Julius family lived near the mouth of the Harbour on a barren group of islets locals referred to as the "Indian Islands," properly the Skardon Islands. The white folks had taken everything else, leaving the Sechelt band as a whole with only four acres of reserve land for each of their drastically reduced numbers, in contrast to the eighty acres per capita provided Native peoples elsewhere in Canada—a gross inequity that caused the Sechelt to start one of the first Native land claims actions, back in the 1880s. In the 2000s they were still hard at work trying to get government action on their grievances.

WHITE SETTLEMENT IN THE HARBOUR WAS shaped by the same factors that shaped the formerly great First Nations community—the excellence of the shelter and the abundance of local fisheries, especially herring. Pender Harbour's herring stocks are fished out now, but they were a natural wonder once. In the words of pioneer Martha Warnock, the place "was polluted with herring, you'd kill a thousand just rowing to the store, clobbering 'em with the oars, you couldn't help it." During my childhood in the 1950s, after two generations of mechanized onslaught by the fishing industry, herring were still so plentiful people used them for pig feed and fertilizer. Jigging a bucket of herring using many-hooked lines or "jigs" baited with embroidery thread was an afternoon ritual on late summer days, and only took a few minutes. You would never bother winding the line in if it only had one or two fish tugging on it; you'd wait until there were eight or ten jerking away and it was too heavy to jig. Then you'd take

Opposite bottom: A surviving net shed in Lee Bay, near the mouth of Pender Harbour. *Keith Thirkell*

Left: The delicious Pacific spot prawn can be sport-fished using traps.

Below: The Pacific spot prawn can grow to ten inches.

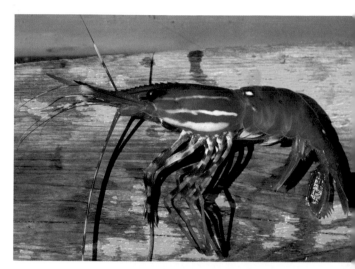

them home and try to talk Gran into making "soused." As my school chum Ted Lee remembered the recipe, the herring were split from the dorsal side and the backbone removed, then covered with black pepper and rolled from the head end. Then they were placed in a baking pan filled with diluted vinegar and baked at a low heat until the bones were soft. Soused herring. It's right up there with wild blackberry pie.

In Native times herring were scooped up using a contraption called a herring rake, which consisted of a long stick bristling with bone needles. In late August just as afternoon was sliding into evening, you could fill a small dugout to the gunwales in a matter of minutes by sweeping the rake through the harbour water in the manner of an oar. What was particularly convenient about herring from the Sechelt point of view was that they spawned in the middle of the winter when clams and dried salmon were starting to get over-familiar. You'd wake up one morning in late February or early March and the harbour shoreline would be plastered for miles with a translucent blanket of sticky, inch-thick roe. If you'd been on your toes you would have hung a bunch of cedar boughs in the water overnight, and they'd be puffed up with roe just as if somebody'd come along and sprayed them with urethane foam. Still today, if you were to show up on the Sechelt band lands with a suitcase full of smoked herring roe on cedar boughs, you could have just about anything you cared to name, short of the McDonald's franchise.

There is a shadowy legend that the first non-Native to occupy the Harbour was a Chinese who in the early 1880s established a fish saltery at the mouth of the Harbour in the area that became known as Irvines Landing after its second settler, a bearded, pipe-smoking Englishman named Charlie Irvine. Irvine built a log-cabin trading post there before leaving it in the hands of the West brothers to take in the Klondike gold rush, then in 1904 sold to the pair who really put Pender Harbour on the map—"Portuguese Joe" Gonzalves and his son-in-law, Theodore (Steve) Dames. Gonzalves and Dames took advantage of the harbour's other chief resource—shelter—and established a full-blown steamer stop complete with deep-sea dock, general store, post office and hotel-saloon. Under their stewardship Pender Harbour became the supply centre for the rich timberlands of the Northern Peninsula–Jervis Inlet–Nelson Island region, and before long other services sprang up. George Duncan started a blacksmith shop in Duncan Cove, and Harry Dusenbury started another one on Dusenbury Island, which also served as the home base for a sealing schooner he owned in partnership with a gnarly old salt named Sandy McLean. According to Gibsons historian Les Peterson, McLean was the original of Wolf Larsen in Jack London's novel *The Sea Wolf,* although I must admit I have at least six others proposed for this honour. A one-armed ex-machinist named Robert Donley established a chicken ranch on Edgecombe Island in 1912, and on October 26 of that year fathered the first male child of European parentage born in the area, William Emmond Donley. Herring continued to play a role, as several salteries brought in their own crews of Scots fishermen, and Donley started a kippering operation and store at his new Donley Landing location. Farming arrived when a family of industrious German immigrants named Klein eyed the sedgy marshland at the head of the harbour and began laboriously erecting hand-built dykes against the tide, planting the salty estuary to sugar beets, berries, spuds and oysters.

Actually the oysters were introduced in 1923 by a Vancouver doctor named MacKechnie who wanted to find something his ne'er-do-well son, Ian, could handle, and thought oysters might be the ticket. These were not the area's natural oysters. Scattered chips of native oyster shell can been found in the middens of old Kalpalin but *Ostea lurida,* the original oyster on

this coast, was so small and scarce as to have limited value as a food source. The larger Pacific oyster, *Crassotrea gigas*, was widely cultivated in Japan, and an experiment in Ladysmith Harbour before the First World War showed it could survive in at least some BC waters.

Dr. MacKechnie was able to buy oyster seed from Japan and plant it on the tidal flats at the head of Pender Harbour, a place now known as Oyster Bay. The idea was just to fatten the oysters for slaughter, since they were not expected to reproduce in the colder BC waters. Ian's job was to oyster-sit, but he found bivalves slow company and began spending his time around the local pub, where trading fresh baking for beer provided more immediate gratification.

Abandoned to their own devices, his oysters found a way to do what comes naturally despite the climatic obstacles and began multiplying in vast numbers. Overnight the local beaches around Pender Harbour took on a scabby appearance not even the eldest Sechelt elder had ever seen before. It was as if there had been a bumper crop of barnacles, except that when you looked closely you found it was dime-sized baby oysters the rocks were plastered with. There was some indignation directed toward that damnfool MacKechnie for making it

Louis Heid's old red barn was always a rarity among the netsheds and log dumps of Pender Harbour.

101

Right: Roosevelt elk have multiplied to the point of becoming a nuisance since being transplanted from Vancouver Island in 1987.
Allan Forest

Below: Giant Pacific oysters of the type encrusting this beach were unknown until being imported from Japan in the 1920s.

so swimmers couldn't find a place to stand that wouldn't cut their feet, and there were many predictions of dire consequences that would come as a result of messing so massively with Mother Nature. But as the dime-sized babies grew to dollar bill-sized adults, people began to believe, even drawing parallels to the story of manna from heaven. The Kleins, whose land surrounded Oyster Bay, soon added oysters to their varied list of cash crops, and oyster picking joined salal picking as a source of survival money for those between paycheques. Visitors from across the water took sackfulls of oysters back to their home beaches, where they continued to multiply, and by the 1950s the entire shoreline of Georgia Strait was studded with the succulent mollusks. Ian MacKechnie meanwhile moved on to other escapades, but he always looked back with pride on his oyster venture, saying it was a runaway success.

Farmland is at a premium around Pender Harbour's rocky shores, but there is some in the Kleindale area.

Like their neighbours to the south, Pender Harbour settlers slowly came around to the realization that forestry was the region's real economic destiny. Small outfits and handloggers probably began fussing at the seaside stands as early as the 1870s, but it wasn't until 1913 that Sweden's answer to perpetual motion, the peripatetic P.B. Anderson, set up 100-man railroad camps in the area, first a few miles south of Pender at Silver Sands, then in the head of the harbour, where he high-graded the towering Douglas-fir forest on the lower slopes of the Caren Range. As a crumbling host of high-notched stumps attest, this was some of the most sublime coniferous forest on the planet, with the kind of Douglas-fir trees author Stewart Holbrook must have been thinking of when he said it would take two good men and a boy just to see all the way to the top of one. It won the Klein family a contract to cut the timber used to create Lumbermen's Arch—an arrangement of colossal fir logs erected in Vancouver's Stanley Park to show just how big trees could get in BC. Lumbermen's Arch became a BC landmark, one of the signatures by which the province was known to the world. By the time the arch began sagging with dry rot a few decades later, there were no replacement logs to be found on the Sunshine Coast. The first-growth giants had all been cut and sent to the mills. The Sechelt Peninsula fir may have been prime in terms of quality, but the quantity was limited in comparison to the stands around Powell River or on Vancouver Island. Today the great armies of loggers who made the place jump to their tune for much of the century have dwindled to a handful of holdouts scrounging runty pecker poles the old-timers would have scorned for fenceposts, and there is only a tree here and there that offers a hint of what the originals might have been like.

As you motor up the highway or cruise along the coast you may spot the odd leaning giant spared by successive generations of fallers because it had "elephant ears"—the big bracket fungus that tells the logger the sturdy-looking trunk is actually riddled with fungus or "conk" within. To get an idea of what a whole forest of such giants might have been like, you can pull off Highway 101 at the Halfmoon–Carlson Forest Service Road just 400 metres south of Trout Lake and take the bumpy road up to the Big Tree Recreation Site parking lot, walk down a charming forest trail and find yourself in a small pocket of virgin Douglas fir averaging about six feet in diameter with one giant pushing eight. By what miracle this stand escaped the faller's axe all these years it is hard to imagine, but all credit to the Sunshine Coast Regional

Bracket fungus on an old mountain hemlock tree.

District for preserving it. Even knowing these trees are but a few isolated survivors, they still exude a cathedral-like power to still the soul with awe. If you can imagine the hills covered with the big sisters of these trees for as far as a day's brisk hike would carry you in any direction, you can get some notion of the forest landscape that confronted the first-comers to the region. Settlers like the Kleins were at first dismayed at the obstacle such trees presented to those whose ultimate aim was to clear the land for farming, but eventually the trees converted them to a different survival strategy—one founded on a rich forest industry. The Klein family survived the death of their farming ambitions to provide the area with some of its classic loggers, renowned for their strength, hard work and unruliness.

At the same time the Harbour attracted its share of the other type of Sunshine Coast settler, the species who valued it for its aesthetic charm.

One of the first settlers seduced by the Harbour's saltgrass spirit was Bertrand W. Sinclair, an author of bestselling westerns who in 1920 homesteaded what has ever since been known as Sinclair Bay. His place became a hot spot for high rollers and made the Harbour a favourite among big-name writers like the spiritualist Stewart Edward White and Erle Stanley Gardner, originator of the Perry Mason industry. Sinclair stayed in Pender Harbour the rest of his life, first switching from writing westerns to novels about BC coast fishing and logging (*Poor Man's Rock*, *The Inverted Pyramid*), then giving up writing altogether to become a full-time salmon troller, which he did into his eighties. I knew him as a barnacled old salt who didn't like to be reminded he'd ever done anything but fish.

The event that earned the Harbour a place of honour on Colombo's Literary Map of Canada did not take place until 1941 when a voluptuous but dispirited-looking twenty-eight-year-old blonde stepped off the *Lady Cynthia* at Irvines Landing and asked if there were a cabin

she might rent for a few months. Bill Matier, the dipsomaniac wharfinger, fixed her up in the old Irvines Landing schoolhouse and tried to make friends, but Elizabeth Smart was preoccupied with other matters. She never explained exactly how she chose Pender Harbour for her nine-month stopover, saying she just stuck a pin in a map, but she must have done enough investigating to determine it had a hospital. Whatever she thought, she was probably directed here by the same forces that washed up all the other eccentrics, for she was surely one.

According to her diary, she came equipped with "trunkfulls of evening dresses and books" and admittedly "knew nothing about practical matters." On her first shopping trip to the Irvines Landing General Store she raised eyebrows by ordering ten pounds of tea, but nothing else that would contribute to a square meal. She couldn't be bothered to keep her stove going in the drafty shack, but played her wind-up phonograph nonstop and plastered her room with cut-out pictures of Madonnas, Christs, and bits of Blake and Ecclesiastes. Police officers who came to look in on her pronounced her "a harmless religious maniac." She had one visitor, a dashing young Brit with a roving eye and a thirst for booze, whom she welcomed by painting her door yellow and decorating her high stilted balcony with dozens of silver cans of bright yellow dandelions, daisies and daffodils. He stayed a few weeks in April, then left her to wander alone along the bush trails and beaches in terrific distress, stumbling about, oblivious to

Massive old-growth Douglas fir at Big Tree Recreation Site are last traces of the coast's original forest.

105

Michael and Dale Jackson started Bluewaters Books in 2009, carrying on the Harbour's strong literary tradition. *Howard White*

others, talking to herself and throwing herself down on the moss and weeping inconsolably. By summer it was clear she was well advanced in pregnancy.

Viv Pieper, the woman behind the counter at the store, blurted out one day, "You're in a bad way, aren't you, my dear? You're in quite a spot?"

"Oh no, thank you, I'm fine."

She tried to give the impression she was married, calling herself "Mrs. Barker," but was franker in her diary, writing on the eve of giving birth to her child, "I hope he will not mind being a bastard. Surely it will help him to avoid the bores, the snobs, the petty, & the afraid."

To local people Smart herself seemed a snob, but nobody could accuse her of being petty or afraid. Raised in a stiflingly proper Upper Canada family, she travelled around the world, lived in a ménage à trois in Mexico, then wound up in an artists' colony at Big Sur, California, where she had the love affair of her life with a fashionable (and married) English poet named George Barker. Barker promised to leave his wife for Smart and did make the one visit to Pender Harbour in April, but only left her more heartbroken than ever. In her diary Smart wrote, "I am dissolved dissolved dissolved with my tears overflowing all Pender Harbour."

She relieved her desperation by pouring it into writing, producing a work of such rhapsodic intensity it has become a classic expression of forsaken love and one of the most celebrated Canadian novels of all time, *By Grand Central Station I Sat Down and Wept.*

Whatever unseen hand had directed Smart to Harbour shores had some years earlier brought another woman who was Smart's match both in cultured background and rebellious spirit. Maximiliane von Upani Southwell was a titled Austrian aristocrat who had chucked the debutante scene in Vienna and somehow ended up living with her invalid husband and ten-year-old son in John Klein's original log cabin at the head of Oyster Bay, "on the dole, but with

Above: In the 1950s, home-grown entrepreneur Olli Sladey built the area's first motel on Gerrans Bay, a site now occupied by upscale Painted Boat Resort. *Howard White*

Right: The former St. Mary's Hospital in Garden Bay, where among other things, the famed writer Elizabeth Smart bore a love-child in 1941.

immense elegance." Southwell of all people could understand what Smart was going through and took the younger woman into her cramped shack, nursing her through the final stages of her book and her pregnancy both. *By Grand Central Station I Sat Down and Wept* was finished just two weeks before Georgina Barker was born in St. Mary's Hospital on August 28, 1941. Though the book gives no credit to "this little place, mostly inhabited by people on the dole, remittance men, etc." for producing the soul-mate who saved the author's life, the novel is dedicated to Maxie Southwell, and they remained lifelong friends.

The two women returned to Pender Harbour in 1970 to revisit the place that inspired Smart to her one flash of genius. They found that her old schoolhouse had been knocked down but that the hospital where Dr. Keith Johnson had delivered the love-child of her legendary affair was still standing, although it had been replaced in 1964 by the present facility in Sechelt. The old hospital building survives today as a sometime heritage resort called the Sundowner Inn. The Kleins' log homestead where Smart finished her book under Maxie Southwell's care survived until recently as an unrecognized literary monument hunching amid the salmonberry canes and surrounded by the tidal mud of Smeshalin from which the Great Spirit had fashioned the first Kalpalin man, according to Sechelt elder Clarence Joe. Alas, it has now been knocked down. As for Maxie, she bought a piece of beachfront next to Hubert Evans in Roberts Creek and spent the rest of her life on the Sunshine Coast, creatively loafing.

These days the balance between those drawn to Pender Harbour mainly for a living and those drawn by the glorious setting has tilted in favour of the latter, although there are plenty who appreciate both. Old-timers are never done marvelling at the way newcomers move in to get away from the city but do their best to bring it with them in the form of lawn sprinkling, high fences, security lights, foreshore leases, and the mindset that goes with all of that.

Bill Thompson's vintage float plane, Garden Bay. *Howard White*

Above: A former cannery cottage survives from the WWI era at Green Bay, Nelson Island.
Howard White

Left: Mountainous Nelson Island with low-lying Hardy Island and Jervis Inlet in the distance.

LEAVING PENDER HARBOUR BY BOAT, THE FIRST thing you bump into is Nelson Island. If you leave by car, you may never hear of it. Nelson Island is the Gulf Island nobody knows even though it's bigger than Bowen, Gabriola or Lasqueti. As a product of Nelson Island myself I have to admit to a bit of a personal hangup about this, one symptom of which is that anything I write longer than five hundred words is likely to mention Nelson Island at least once. But I'm not the only one to experience a twinge of defensiveness. Local historian Karen Southern, when preparing her excellent little book, *The Nelson Island Story*, at first considered calling it *Not Just a Lot of Rock and Christmas Trees*. I have been trying to think up a book to go with that title ever since.

Float planes make life possible in the unroaded parts of the Sunshine Coast.

Those who deny Nelson Island its rightful place often claim nobody lives there. In fact, Nelson has been continuously occupied about as long as any other part of the Sunshine Coast, at least since the early 1890s when an English schoolteacher named John Wray landed with his wife, Sarah, and five children at Hidden Bay on the west side of the island. True, the advantages of Nelson Island life were not apparent to Sarah immediately, but she was a town girl born and bred whose entire wilderness experience before following her husband into darkest British Columbia consisted of two visits to the English seashore. One day when John came home from getting the mail (obviously no five-minute chore), he found her waiting with all their possessions packed and an ultimatum on her lips: "I want to get out of here right now." John must have been a good talker. He moved, but only a few miles down the beach to Quarry Bay, where the granite quarry offered steady wages and at least some society. Forty years later John and Sarah were still married and still living on Nelson Island, progenitors of a numerous clan that did much to tame the Sunshine Coast.

The full-time Nelson population has not always been able to claim quantity, the average being somewhere under twenty-five, but quality ought to count for something. I have already mentioned that this was the island Harry Roberts sought refuge on after fleeing the over-development of Roberts Creek in 1930. One of his neighbours was a sister of the outlaw Jesse James, who is remembered for firing shots across the bow of the steamer *Comox* when she wanted it to call on her rancherie near Quarry Bay. (Most settlers were satisfied simply to hoist a flag.)

Nelson Island has not lacked for major industries, although things have slowed since the end of World War I. It may be all rock and Christmas trees, but the rock is damn fine rock. The island's earliest developers made a virtue of adversity by turning the whole west side of the island into a series of stone quarries, and Nelson Island granite found its way into the Vancouver Art Gallery, both Vancouver post offices, the BC legislative buildings and a million or so headstones.

The island had a salmon cannery once, down near Green Bay on the east side, which is curious since there are no major salmon runs in that neighbourhood. Ian MacKechnie, the oyster pioneer, explained it to me by pointing out that during a world war "you can can anything that swims." His view is supported by the fact that at the war's end the cannery was quickly converted into a shingle mill, then later into an extremely low budget summer resort. This was not the island's first tourist facility. Back near the turn of the century a visionary named John West had built a seventeen-room hotel on Agamemnon Channel, which he christened Westmere Lodge. On opening night he had one guest, and it went downhill from there. Later reports find Mr. West sawing his hotel in half and using the lumber thus liberated to heat the remaining half. Island people are not always practical, but they are tenacious. The good half of Westmere Lodge is still functioning.

Leaving Pender Harbour by car, you follow Highway 101 around the Peninsula's largest and most popular lakes, Sakinaw and Ruby, before pausing for another ferry ride at Earls Cove, once the homestead of the Earl family, whom I remember for nothing so much as their amazing way of talking. Living alone in a place that was a paragon of wilderness isolation before the government abruptly turned it into a mass transit depot, the Earls developed one of the most picturesque drawls to be encountered this side of the Ozarks. Come to think of it, their neighbour Olli Sladey, the Sechelt Peninsula's first millionaire, had a way of squeezing all the juice out of his vowels, too. It gives you an inkling of how quickly a local dialect can get started. The Earl boys' parents were English and Olli's Finnish, but by the time civilization caught up with them halfway through their second generation on the site, the two families were well on their way to concocting a new variety of spoken English. There was lots of that in the old days. The fishermen in Pender Harbour had their own sound. The gillnetters, that

Sakinaw (below) and Ruby are the two largest lakes on the Baja Sunshine Coast.

Above: The Earls Cove–Saltery Bay ferry across Jervis Inlet joins the two halves of the Sunshine Coast.

Above right:
Old fishboat, Egmont.
Keith Thirkell

Right: A "zunga" hanging from a big arbutus.
Keith Thirkell

is. Net-men were more communal, whereas the trollers, being off by themselves most of the time, tended to develop one-man dialects. People from different areas would invent their own words. One I remember from Powell River is *zunga*, for the rope you use to swing out over a swimming hole. Everybody up there says it, but I never heard it anywhere else.

EGMONT, A VILLAGE OF ABOUT 250 DOWN a three-mile side road just before the ferry terminal, is something of a throwback to a time of traditional gumboot customs though even here, modern currents are fast erasing the old sounds, smells and sights.

Like Pender Harbour and so many of the smaller, older settlements, Egmont was made up of big, extended families—the Jeffries, the Silveys, the Griffiths, the Vaughans, the Wests. The Silveys especially, descendants of a Portuguese trader named Joseph Silvey who ran the second saloon in Vancouver and in 1868 fathered the first child with European content born in that city, personify the community's distinctive salal brush roots.

Egmont is also like Pender Harbour in the way it defies rational town planning by rambling along the beach from bay to point to cove, as roads twist and turn maniacally to keep up. Egmont is a little like one of those prairie towns bisected by rail yards, except in this case the divider is a busy marine thoroughfare called Sechelt Narrows. Old Egmont on the north side

Following pages: Hotham Sound offers a good fjord experience for those without time or boat enough to tackle Jervis Inlet.

The government wharf at Egmont.

113

Right: Skookumchuck Rapids at Egmont has some of the fastest tidal currents on the planet.

Below: The tidal rapids at Sechelt Narrows, a.k.a. "The Skookumchuck," needs to be seen on a big tide to be appreciated.

of the inlet is accessible only by water, giving docks, boardwalks, beaching grids, kicker boats and water taxis a prominence that recalls the earlier days of many coastal communities. A careful observer will note that Egmont's waterfront has a somewhat more battened-down look in comparison to Pender, owing to the heavy currents flowing in and out of Skookumchuck Rapids, just down the inlet.

The Skookumchuck experience, along with touring Princess Louisa Inlet (also accessible from Egmont), is one of the must-do's of visiting the Sunshine Coast, although it can be rather anti-climactic if you don't time your visit to catch a big tide at full rip. Even then, it may strike you as not much different than a patch of moderately white water on a medium-sized river. What the chuck does that no river does is slam into reverse every six hours, and you can't experience its full eeriness without observing a whole cycle from spin to soak to spin again. Even that is nothing beside the death-defying thrill of venturing into its smoking maw in some sort of vessel, keeping in mind that about a dozen people that we know of have died doing this. The total is likely to keep increasing as the chuck grows more popular with whitewater kayakers and other addicts of the extreme.

Deluxe lodgings at West Coast Wilderness Lodge, Egmont. *Keith Thirkell*

4
JERVIS INLET

JERVIS INLET, WHICH ZIGZAGS DEEP into the Coast Range like a forty-mile light-ning bolt between the Peninsula and the Powell River side, is a classic coastal fjord, shad-owed most of its length by mile-high mountain walls. It is very deep. A marker buoy is anchored about mid-stream offshore of St. Vincent Bay, and you often see pleasure boats giving it a wide berth, no doubt thinking that, like most marker buoys, this one must in-dicate treacherous shallows. In fact it indicates the greatest depth of water to be found on the Inside Passage, a 3,000-foot hole known as "the Jervis Deep." It is marked because the US military at one time confiscated it for testing deep-water weaponry.

Previous pages: Vancouver Bay in Jervis Inlet is surrounded by precipitous mountains.

The *Malibu Princess* plies the waters of Jervis Inlet transporting summer campers to and from the spectacular Malibu Club.

Actually I think of this wide gulf between the mainland and Nelson Island as pre-inlet, although it's shown on the maps as all one with Jervis. It's not until you round Foley Head and begin ascending the long crack in the mountains that you start getting that claustrophobic feeling I associate with the real Jervis Inlet. As the nervous skipper I am, I always find this part of the inlet a little menacing from the vantage point of a small boat. Just as Howe Sound has a resident typhoon called the Squamish, Jervis has an even meaner one called the Jervis Express and it has a habit of cooking up on short notice. The sheer cliffs afford no shelter, and the inlet's deep bottom is littered with rickety camp tenders, fishboats and the bones of luckless gyppo loggers who failed to show proper respect for the volatile local weathers. There are a few places where the steep-to shores relax into a brief dent of river mouth, at Vancouver Bay, Brittain River and Deserted Bay, but even these places offer dubious refuge.

The parts of Jervis that are not bare granite bluff speckled with moun-tain goats were once thickly forested with fir and cedar, but now offer a case study in the effects of bad logging practices. The hillsides above Egmont Point at the entrance to the inlet proper have regained some of their green cover after being clear-cut thirty or forty years ago, but a mass of ugly brown washouts that snake down sometimes five hundred feet bear witness to the risks involved in building logging roads on steep slopes. On the opposite side of the inlet great barren patches can be seen where the timber has failed to regenerate three decades after logging, and the hillside north of Brittain River remains scruffy from a logging-related forest fire in the 1950s. Elsewhere, in the broad valleys of the Vancouver and Deserted rivers, the great Douglas-fir stands that spawned big rail-way camps early in the century have surged back with such profusion the sites are choked with stunted, undersized timber that is prey to a host of diseases and parasites. It was to bring an end to such environmental degradation that the provincial NDP govern-ment clamped down on destructive logging practices with its Forest Practices Code in 1995, which was promptly repealed and replaced with the more industry-friendly Forest and Range Practices Act in 2004.

120

Above: Purple sea stars love to party.

Left: The sheer walls of Jervis Inlet can take your breath away.

Far left: The inlets of the Sunshine Coast offer some of the most scenic boating in the world.

121

Above: Chatterbox Falls is the focal point of scenic Princess Louisa Inlet.

Left: Reflected magnificence, Princess Louisa Inlet. *Keith Thirkell*

The beauties of Princess Louisa Inlet defy description.

THE FEATURE THAT SETS JERVIS APART FROM ITS sister inlets occurs ten miles from the head on the east side. There the mountain walls unexpectedly part and let into a four-mile side inlet surrounded by such precipitous bluffs the effect is like looking up at the sky from the bottom of a colossal and extremely gorgeous cavern. "There is no use describing that inlet," Erle Stanley Gardner once wrote, before proceeding to ignore his own advice. "There is a calm tranquility which stretches from the smooth surface of the reflecting waters straight up into infinity. The deep calm of eternal silence is only disturbed by the muffled roar of throbbing waterfalls as they plunge down from sheer cliffs. There is no scenery in the world that can beat it. Not that I've seen the rest of the world. I don't need to. I've seen Princess Louisa Inlet."

I won't fall into the trap of trying to describe Princess Louisa except to say few Sunshine Coasters would deny it is the Hope Diamond of the area's scenic jewels. It is the place we take those special visitors we want to hook on the coast, the one experience guaranteed to jar the most jaded soul into a full-blown state of awe. I have been visiting Princess Louisa regularly since I was a kid and it never seems enough. Despite going in many different weathers, moods and ages, it has never failed to send me away with a renewed sense of life's promise.

The inlet's rare magnetism draws remarkable people to it and inspires them to extraordinary exertions. Legend has it that it was avoided by the Sechelt after a small village at the head was buried by one of the inlet's periodic rockslides, but band elder Clarence Joe told me his people used to visit it for recreational purposes just as the white man would later.

Princess Louisa was ignored by the muckers early on because its only substantial resource

124

Kids get a chance to experience the wilderness at Malibu Camp.

was beauty, which didn't readily lend itself to being canned or milled—a challenge inventor Thomas Hamilton would apply himself to later.

Herman Casper just wanted to wake up in the morning and see it. Casper was a deserter from the German army who homesteaded the only decently flat land in the area, the peninsula down at the inlet mouth by Malibu Rapids, in 1900. When he wasn't blacksmithing for local handloggers, Casper whiled away his days spoiling his twenty-six cats and composing songs in praise of the magnificent surroundings, which he was happy to perform with his zither for visiting boaters:

Beyond Mount Alfred, in ze vest
Where ze sun goes down to rest
It draws me dere, I don' know vy
S'pose it is ze colour in ze sky.
For zey are purple, mauve and pink
Howeber it makes me vunder, look, and t'ink.

Casper was followed by Charles (Daddy) Johnstone, a towering mountain man from Daniel Boone country who kept edging west ahead of civilization until he and his six family landed up at Princess Louisa around 1909. There they threw together a one-room split-cedar shack, lived off the land and had three more kids. The Johnstone gang may have succeeded in

125

getting closer to the inlet's soul than anyone since the Sechelt in the days when they had it to themselves. As part of their education, the old man used to send sons, Steve and Judd, up on the snowy plateau above Princess Louisa without jacket or shoes and only matches, salt and a jackknife for survival. They would live by their wits for weeks at a time, and explore miles into the interior of the province. After World War I, Daddy began to feel even Jervis was too cramped and carried on to Alaska, where he became famous as a pioneer. But Steve and Judd returned and passed the rest of their days in homage to the fabulous Jervis landscape that had been so deeply imprinted on them in their formative years. Their names became synonymous with the inlet's wild spirit and Judd in particular became famous for his tall tales of pioneer times.

Judd married Dora Jeffries from Egmont and stayed up Princess Louisa through the birth of their first three girls, sixty miles from the nearest family. The sun would disappear behind the inlet crags for two months in the depths of winter and it would get so cold the salt water would freeze from shore to shore. To get anything that couldn't be obtained from the bush Judd would have to drag the boat across two miles of sea ice and row to Pender Harbour, a hundred-mile round trip. He was always a welcome sight at Portuguese Joe's bar in Irvines Landing and never had to pay for a drink. All you had to do was ask him how things were going.

A brave oystercatcher holds its own in a clutch of gulls.

"Could be worse. Had a hard blow and a cedar tree come down on the shack is all."

"Very big?"

"Naw, only about six foot on the butt."

"Good God, Judd. Didn't it do a lot of damage?"

"Naw. Fell crost the bed right where the old woman was sleepin', but it hung up on the stove before it could git 'er. Tore the roof off is all."

"That's terrible, Judd!"

"Naw. I just took a couple blocks off the end and split up a mess o' shakes. Old woman bin after me fer a new roof anyways."

"What about the rest of the tree. How did you remove it?"

"Didn't bother. It was pointin' in the stove anyways, so I jus' lit the fire and stuck the Gilchrist jack on the other end. Every time the old woman wanted some exter heat, I just hollered at the kid to go out and give a few clicks on the jack. It was auto-feed, like."

"So it wasn't so bad after all."

"Hell no. I got a new roof and a whole winter's heat without once havin' to leave the shack."

I sometimes wonder if it was due to Judd Johnstone that the entire Jervis Inlet–Nelson Island area seemed to become such a prime bullshit-producing zone. When I was growing up there it seemed you couldn't get a straight answer out of anybody.

Certainly you couldn't get one out of James (Mac) Macdonald, the globetrotting American playboy who fell under the Princess's spell in 1919. "After travelling around the world and seeing many of its famous beauty spots, I felt I was well able to evaluate the magnificence of Princess Louisa," he wrote in one of his more sober utterances. "This place had to equal or better anything I had seen."

Sea blush carpets mossy slopes near the shoreline.

127

Like many another wealthy American who no sooner spied a thing of beauty in a foreign land than he had to have it, Macdonald promptly applied to the BC government to purchase the inlet head, and the government turned out to be eager to unload it. Their appraisal of the 292-acre site, which would come to be called "The Eighth Wonder of the World" and attract 20,000 gawkers a season despite its inaccessibility, was that only 42 acres were flat enough to be of any use, so Macdonald could have the whole thing for $420, if that wasn't asking too much. He took possession in 1927.

Through absolutely no fault of its own, this turned out to be the best thing the government could have done. Within a few years Macdonald would be turning down $400,000 offers from hotel chains and preserving the area for public use with a determination the government would not come to appreciate until 1964, when Macdonald finally had the satisfaction of seeing his beloved charge consecrated as a Class A Marine Park.

Rich, eloquent and handsome, "Mac" Macdonald could have had his pick of successful careers, but from his fateful encounter with the Princess in the prime of his life until the day he could no longer hobble around on his own, he devoted his entire existence to being

Forest trail, Princess Louisa Marine Park.

her chief admirer, protector and ambassador to the world. He got married in 1939, but the new wife made the mistake of forcing him to choose between the Princess and her, and a Mexican divorce quickly followed.

Mac left the inlet only during the winter months, when the weather becomes much harsher than the coastal norm. At first he rented a *pied à terre* in Pender Harbour from his friend Bertrand Sinclair, and later he established regular winter digs in Acapulco. From May to October he was back at Princess Louisa, continuing his endless study of her moods, cataloguing her wonders and expounding on them to visitors. In time every feature in the inlet, from Chatterbox Falls to Trapper's Rock, came to be known by a name Mac gave it. He became a walking encyclopedia of inlet history and lore, most of it unreliable, but all of it highly entertaining.

Macdonald's presence became an attraction in itself, compelling regulars like John Barrymore to return year after year to pass long evenings sitting on the afterdeck of his splendiferous MV *Infanta*, where Mac would tell stories and point out faces in the rock formations of the bluffs. (Barrymore claimed to have discovered Napoleon, though Mac later speculated you had to be drinking Napoleon brandy to see it.) Hollywood types seemed to take a particular shine to Mac. At various times he entertained the likes of Ronald Colman, William Powell, and Mack Sennett, complete with his entourage of bathing beauties, who filmed part of a movie called *Alaskan Love Song* in the inlet, but he was equally attentive to locals and kids, reputedly turning down dinner with Arthur Godfrey so he could keep a storytelling date at the youth camp. This is all the more notable considering Mac's legendary appetite for free grub. It is said that from the time the first yacht showed up in the spring to the time the last one left in the fall, he never ate his own cooking.

Macdonald was a great admirer of Judd Johnstone and, after Judd moved south to Hardy Island, of his brother Steve, who stayed up-inlet all his life. He was also a great fan of old Casper. During one of his winters south, Macdonald hired some professional musicians to make a record of Casper's songs, which proved a great hit among inlet fanciers and netted the old smithy a rare spot of cash. Macdonald was outraged in 1940 when aviation tycoon Thomas Hamilton talked Casper into parting with his beloved acreage for $500 so he could build a luxury resort called Malibu Lodge. Mac cheered when Malibu went broke in 1947 and was taken over by Young Life, a non-denominational church group offering low-budget vacations to city kids.

Macdonald was particularly attentive to Muriel Blanchet, the adventuring Victoria widow who cruised the inlet with her five children in the 1930s. With the help of Hubert Evans she recorded her experiences in the coastal classic *The Curve of Time*, which has a lengthy passage describing Mac as "the Man from California," which of course he wasn't. He also kept up a kind of friendly bullshitting competition with Tom Brazil, caretaker of the Macomber estate on Hardy Island down south at the mouth of Jervis Inlet, who had a troupe of tame deer and entertained boaters with a repertoire of tall tales and bogus lore that rivalled Mac's. Mac would arrange for southbound boaters to stop in and give Brazil the latest news from Princess Louisa—for instance, that Mac had narrowly escaped being killed by a cougar which leapt at him from behind a tree and would have got him but for Mac's quick side-jump, an uncanny move he had perfected in his college football days. Following the attack, the story went, Mac heard some crashing in the bush, and here was the cougar, hopping back and forth practising his football move.

Brazil would have a few days to think about that before sending the next boat north with the latest news from Hardy Island, perhaps about his bear, the one he had raised from a cub and taught to do odd jobs around the place. In fact he had nicknamed this bear "Mac," because it was so effective mooching grub from visiting boats. One day he needed the bear to skid a wood log out of the bush, but call as he would, he couldn't raise it. Then he saw something big and black rooting around in a berry patch and whistled the special signal that meant "time to saddle up," but the bear ignored him. Tom had to beat it on the snout with a knotty fir branch before he could climb on its back, and even then the bear proved to be in such an ornery mood he could hardly stay aboard. They were both covered with lumps by the time they finally got the log skidded down to the woodshed. No sooner were they unhitched than another bear came staggering out of the shed and gave Tom a big lick on the face. It was only then he realized his pet bear had been sleeping in the woodshed the whole time. The one he'd been riding was a wild one that had strayed by.

Sometimes Mac would resort to composing his ripostes on paper. On September 12, 1941, he sent a boat down-inlet carrying this letter:

My Dear Mr. Brazil,
Last week I had a visit from Corp. Allen of Powell River who stated that he had visited Hardy Island recently and that while he was walking across the island he had seen a peculiar looking animal half man and half beast lurking in the woods. The Corporal immediately concluded that it must be one of your African offspring that was visiting you—and not wishing to embarrass you did not mention the matter to you. I questioned the Corporal concerning the man-beast and immediately realized that it was my very valuable Orang-utan which I had imported from Sumatra several years ago at great expense.

As I am growing into the sunset years of life and no longer have the strength or stamina to climb the mountains and milk the wild goats before breakfast, I have trained this animal to perform that chore for me, so you can readily understand how much I miss my Orang-utan and how tired I am getting of canned milk.

Now Mr. Brazil, I am not accusing you of theft for I know you to be a man of upright character—at least, that is the reputation your children have given you, and I have met a lot of them in the South Seas, China, Africa, and in Borneo. How you obtained my Orang-utan I don't know, but I want you to return him *immediately*. I suggest that you have him properly caged and charter a boat and send him up here accompanied by Mr. Forrest (Judd) Johnstone or some other reputable animal trainer. If you send Mr. Johnstone along with my animal please put a label around Mr. Johnstone's neck so that I shall know which is the Orang-utan.

Very truly yours,

James Macdonald

A harbour seal dives for safety. Once reduced by bounty hunting, seal numbers have rebounded along the coast.

Under the inlet's influence Macdonald became one of the most ardent apostles of the creed that humanity was placed on the Sunshine Coast "not to be doing but to be." He even went so far as to dedicate himself formally to "the satisfying state of loaferhood."

"The world needs ten million full time thinking loafers dedicated to the purpose of bringing this cockeyed life back to its normal balance," he declared in his five-point manifesto of loaferdom.

Of course it helped to be the favourite son of a Seattle grocery heiress, a fact Macdonald made no bones about, advising would-be loafers: "Before birth, look the field over and pick out a family in which some member has misspent his life in amassing sufficient do-re-me to permit you to dodge the squirrel cage." In this he differs from the Johnstone boys, who would argue that you could enjoy the best the coast had to offer with no more accumulated assets than a jackknife and a box of matches.

I remember Mac as a pleasant old man with a crown of luminous silver hair who used to keep his houseboat, the *Seaholm*, in Madeira Park while he waited for the inlet to thaw in the spring. I had a paper route, and while it was a bit of nuisance to paddle over to where he was anchored, it was always worth seeing what nonsense he would come up with. One spring he launched into a big production about a new sport which had taken Acapulco beaches by storm that season, and ceremoniously produced this wonderful innovation he'd smuggled back just for my benefit. I was excited by the buildup but disappointed by the actual item, which looked like the lid off a small garbage can. He said you flicked it so it sort of hovered like a flying saucer. He made me practise it with him until I had the knack, then commanded me to go off and spread the fad among my friends. That was how Madeira Park became the first Canadian beachhead of the Frisbee craze, way back in 1957. To a twelve-year-old, Mac seemed like nothing so much as a great big overaged kid, which I am sure is a judgment he would have been most delighted to accept. The only thing you had to watch is that he didn't lure you inside his cabin and try to make you play chess. As a chess fanatic he was known for his willingness to play with anyone, no matter how incompetent, but I am sad to say even his legendary patience was checkmated in my case.

Mac died in a Seattle rest home in 1978. His ashes are planted inside a boulder at the head of Princess Louisa, beneath an inscription that reads "Laird of the inlet, Gentleman, friend to all who came here."

A peaceful day in Jervis Inlet.

5

THE POWELL RIVER AREA

A FRIEND OF MINE WHO WORKS for one of the big forest companies had to travel up the coast recently explaining some new joint government–industry strategy and was quite struck with the difference between the north side of Jervis Inlet and the south in attitudes about logging and industrial progress in general. The meetings on the lower coast were big noisy affairs overflowing with well-prepared critics of all philosophical shades, where the upper coast meetings were small, businesslike and supportive.

Palm Beach near Lang Bay is the site of a music festival that marked its 30th anniversary in 2011. *Darren Robinson*

"Boy that's a cranky area you live in," she said rather accusingly, as if harbouring a suspicion I might be part of the problem (completely unfounded). She came to the meeting prepared for a barrage of green-think, which she got, but was blindsided by a bellicose business agent for the loggers' union who attacked her for being too green herself. "They were coming at us from every direction," she said. "But it's a different world up Powell River way. They like jobs up there."

To cross over to the north side of the inlet is to leave the spirit of genteel loaferdom behind. The forty-mile coastline between the ferry dock at Saltery Bay and the terminus of Highway 101 at Lund, which local residents break into some ten distinct communities while lower coasters lump them all together as Powell River, is presided over by an industrious spirit that tends to be impatient with those who lack the Protestant work ethic. This is perhaps unavoidable given the great resource wealth of the area, which has made it much more of an industrial zone than the lower coast. My father has always maintained that Powell River is a better place to live than the crank-infested lower coast, but given that he thinks both Harry Roberts and Mac Macdonald were self-regarding layabouts, I suppose that isn't too surprising.

The Jervis Inlet ferry is worth taking just for the scenic experience. *Keith Thirkell*

The principal determining factor in Powell River history is that broad stretch of low-elevation real estate lying inland of the coast between Stillwater and Lund, roughly forty miles square, which supported a forest comparable in quality to that on the Sechelt Peninsula but vaster in volume.

From the 1890s onward the Powell Forest attracted many of the major forest companies of the time, including the venerable Hastings Mill Company of Vancouver at Lang Bay and Wildwood; Bloedel, Stewart & Welch of Bellingham at Myrtle Point; Lamb Lumber Company then Brooks, Scanlon & O'Brien of Minnesota at Stillwater; and Merrill & Ring of Seattle in Theodosia Inlet. Between 1896 and 1955, when the Eagle River and Northern Railway pulled up the area's last functioning trackage, the Powell River area was one of the great centres of steam railway logging, with 20 locomotives and 300 cars running on over 100 miles of track. Camps in the area housed more than a thousand men. Little trace of this activity remains except enormous crumbling stumps and an old steam locomotive reputed to be rusting in

134

Freil Falls in Hotham Sound is one of the scenic highlights on the Jervis Inlet ferry crossing.

Powell Riverites know how
to enjoy their surroundings.
Keith Thirkell

peace somewhere beyond the head of Lewis Lake. The timber giant Western Forest Products still operates its Stillwater Division and Andy Byrne's Granet Lake show keeps another couple dozen off the street, but the total complement of loggers still active in the area has likely dwindled to fewer than two hundred.

Just the same, the area still carries the stamp of the big timber era on its soul. At the turn of the century, as settlers from the Gibson family down at Gibsons Landing to the Thulins up at Lund were consolidating their footholds in the coastal forest, the stretch of shoreline where Powell River and Westview repose today was unsettled slash. Across Malaspina Strait, Texada Island was booming with its twin cities of Van Anda and Texada City, and up the coast at Lund the Thulin brothers were already building their second hotel, but the only permanent resident along the Powell River shore was a squatter from Missouri named Tom Ogburn. Ogburn had crisscrossed the continent looking for the perfect wilderness home, and circa 1900 he built his log cabin at the top of the falls on Powell River.

Poor Tom. In 1907 he woke up to find a railroad rumbling past his back door as the Michigan and Puget Logging Company established their pioneering 2.5-mile line from the lake to the beach, later extended to what is now known as Willingdon Beach Park. But even that disturbance would soon seem minor. In 1908 the Brooks Scanlon company decided the area's vast timber wealth, combined with the hydroelectric potential of the spectacular falls that

136

thundered undammed onto the beach, made Powell River a likely spot to establish one of western Canada's first pulp and paper mills. Tom's cabin was soon in the middle of a roaring construction site as the newly formed Powell River Company stripped the little valley to build its dam, mill and townsite. Unlike unsuccessful attempts at Swanson Bay and Port Mellon, the Powell River pulp mill was a winner, and after some early struggles, rapidly grew into the largest pulp and paper mill in the world, creating a prosperous new coastal city around it. By the 1940s, the bountiful local timber supply that had provided the original impetus for the mill was petering out, but the enterprise had enough momentum that it was pulling fibre in from all parts of the coast. Between 1921 and 1941 the town grew from 2,100 to 8,000 people; by 1981 it peaked at over 20,000.

This dramatic development overshadowed everything else that took place in the whole region. It does still, although the area is undergoing a kind of slow shift away from primary industry that is taking place everywhere else on BC's south coast. Modernization and a dwindling fibre supply have reduced the mill workforce to a fraction of what it was twenty years ago, which still makes it the largest single employer in town but leaves it less dominant in the local economy. Meanwhile the area is being discovered by the retirees and refugees from the Lower Mainland who like the great infrastructure and affordable real estate.

The Powell River paper mill is still the town's largest employer, but downsizing has eroded its once-dominant position.

Right: The old courthouse building in the lower townsite recalls Powell River's days as a company town.

Below: The old Powell River General Hospital.

THE MOST UNUSUAL SIGHT IN SALTERY BAY AT the start of the drive into Powell River can't be viewed from the highway, or from a boat, or from anything but a wetsuit. It is a nine-foot bronze statue of a mermaid and it is located three fathoms under the sea just off-shore of the Saltery Bay Campsite. It didn't fall off the ferry—it was placed there on purpose to anchor Powell River's not uncontested claim to being the "Scuba Diving Capital of Canada." The area running from Saltery Bay to Thunder Bay has long been a hot spot for underwater sightseeing, boasting an "Octopus City" and several wrecks as well as the bra-less bronze. If you want to check, you don't have to be Jacques Cousteau. This dive site is advertised as wheelchair accessible.

After snaking around the notorious Thunder Bay bluffs, the road levels out and traverses a gently sloping landscape with a southerly exposure that was surveyed into forty-acre parcels back in the 1920s when the government was still clinging to the idea that the highest use it could be put to was farming. In the words of the late Paradise Valley pioneer Roy Padgett, "They were selling it for two and a half dollars an acre for years before they realized this was forest land with second-growth timber on it worth thousands to the acre." Occasional green fields can still be seen holding out against the relentless onslaught of temperate jungle. One of the first and grandest of the forest farms can be glimpsed just as the road comes down off the bluffs where in the late 1890s Farquar McRae homesteaded most of the lush 1,500-acre peninsula that runs out to wave-swept Scotch Fir Point. He wrestled the great fir stumps out of the soil until he, like the Kleins, realized there was less money in slaughtering his beeves than in hitching them to trees, and so turned ox-logger. Three-quarters of a century of selective logging by Farquar and his son, Fraser, left the vast McCrae spread more or less intact and a lot of hearts were broken when it was not made into a park after Fraser's passing. It would have given the south coast another Lighthouse Park.

A couple of miles farther along, the highway affords a close-up view of one of the coast's most familiar landmarks, the Stillwater surge tank. The twenty-storey structure balances pressure in the mile-long penstock that carries water from the dam on Lois Lake down to the Powell River mill's auxiliary powerhouse on Stillwater Bay. Because of its placement on the hillside with full exposure to Malaspina Strait, mariners can sight the Stillwater tower clear down to Bellingham. Small boaters steering courses up the gulf have become so dependent on it as a landmark over the years that if it is ever discontinued as a surge tank, it will have to be kept up as an aid to navigation.

The Powell Forest is positively sodden with lakes and Lois River, emptying the Lois Lake–Khartoum Lake–Horseshoe Lake system, is the second-largest drainage after the Powell Lake system itself. As you whiz over the concrete viaduct that spans the Lois River gorge just a mile past the surge tank, you may wonder at stories like the one pioneer Edith Flynn told about crossing this river as a child: "The first bridge across the river was just below the present bridge, at the first curve in the river below the falls. It was made from two logs, one larger one on the high side and one smaller one on the low side so you were walking on a tilt, and it had a belly in the middle so it sloped up to the bank on either end. It was quite scary, because it was very high, and it would wobble. It had a handrail, but you didn't dare lean on it. I saw

One of the more renowned sights in the Powell River area is located sixty feet underwater at Mermaid Cove, near Saltery Bay. It is a nine-foot bronze sculpture by Simon Morris called "The Emerald Princess" and was placed by local scuba enthusiasts.
Top: Jim Willoughby /
Above: Darren Robinson

Above: The surge tank at Stillwater, used to even out flow into the hydro turbines, serves as an unofficial daymark for passing boaters.

Right: Rainy Day Lake. The Powell River area is blessed with an abundance of recreational lakes.
Darren Robinson

people start out walking, then get down on their hands and knees, then get scared to go any further. We kids got so used to it we didn't think anything of it." You may look over the edge of the new Lois River bridge and search in vain for the raging torrent the early settlers called the Eagle River, which once drained three lakes called the Gordon Pashas. When a wooden crib dam was built at the outlet of the first Gordon Pasha in 1930 and then replaced by a higher concrete dam in 1942, the two lower lakes were merged into one large one renamed Lois Lake. This lake serves as the jumping-off point for the Powell Forest canoe route, a spectacular and extremely well-established forty-mile course that loops through twelve lakes and comes out on Powell Lake just above the river. At the same time Lois Lake was created, the river draining it was renamed the Lois River, but the name was somewhat academic since most of the water was diverted through the Stillwater penstock, leaving barely enough moisture in the old channel to wet the gravel on most days.

Either way, the water still finds its way to tidewater at Stillwater, today a tiny hamlet that impresses one as having deep roots in the past. Starting in 1909, this was the base of some of the area's largest logging operations, when the US firm Brooks, Scanlon & O'Brien built a railway system reaching twenty miles back into the fabulously rich timber of the Eagle (Lois) River drainage. The land around the Gordon Pasha chain was logged using fifteen steam donkeys and two large floating camps, which were towed from claim to claim. Stillwater served as the social centre of the mainland side before the Powell River mill was established in 1911, and had a hotel, store and community hall to go with the big BS&O'B camp. It was this

Left: The Shinglemill Pub and Restaurant at Powell Lake.

Below: Summer fun at Stillwater bluffs. *Darren Robinson*

company that got the bright idea of starting the pulp and paper mill that changed the history of the whole region.

A few miles farther north Highway 101 crosses a smaller watercourse known as Lang Creek, which is still full of water and each fall is packed with hatchery-produced salmon. Lang Creek drains the third-largest of the area's lake systems, Haslam Lake, and was the site of the area's first logging railway, established sometime in the 1890s by the pioneering Hastings Mill Company of Vancouver. This company was succeeded by the legendary Lamb Lumber Company, whose redoubtable leader, John Blacklock "Daddy" Lamb, was a frustrated farmer famous for getting settlers to start stump ranches in the logged-off slash along his railroads. If you want the thrill of running the family Hupmobile over one of the area's oldest logging railway beds, Zilinsky Road at Lang Bay follows the grade of Lamb's old Vancouver Timber and Trading Company Railway. This line was unique in that it was the only one of the area's big pioneer logging operations that was not operated by an American company. In 1916, the Haslam Lake Timber and Logging Company Railway, a longer line, was run up the opposite side of Lang Creek to Haslam Lake and used to load out logs dumped into the lake by operations all around its shores.

The Lang Creek–Kelly Creek–Black Point area offered the most attractive land along this

Haslam Lake, third-largest of Powell River's many lakes, was the site of the area's first logging railway.
Darren Robinson

Pasture land in the Black Point area. *Keith Thirkell*

shore, resulting in some of the more permanent homesteading experiments. It still retains some of the feeling of an independent community, with its own community hall and a charming picnic ground fronting the fabulous Palm Beach.

There is something uniquely striking about Myrtle Point, about five miles closer to Powell River, and it's not only that the road breaks out of the bush and at last offers the traveller a more than fleeting glimpse of Malaspina Strait. It may be the area's history. White settlement at Myrtle Point harks back before logging to the era of the fur trade, when a fur trader named Leonard Frolander set up a trading post in the 1880s, arguably the first non-Native settlement along the Powell River shore. Frolander held sway into the late 1890s, then in 1911 the big Seattle firm Bloedel, Stewart & Welch chose the site as the saltwater base for a sprawling logging enterprise that would involve five camps stretching from nearby Paradise Valley to the side of Mount Smith at the head of Haslam Lake, twenty miles away.

Myrtle Point is one of the only big camp locations from the glory days of steam logging where you can still see some outlines of the old works. The little islets offshore still carry remnants of the rock fill used to create a breakwater for the big BS&W booming ground, and lines of black posts in the beach mud—the stumps of rotted pilings—trace a ghostly outline of the elaborate railway trestle that used to carry the four locomotives and fifty-three log cars of the BS&W railroad out to the log dump. The flat peninsula on the shore side of the highway still bears the footprint of one of the most storied pioneer camps on the coast, where world-heavyweight-champion-to-be Jack Dempsey worked as a green chokerman in the early years of the century. The scraps of rusty logging equipment lying about date from more recent operations, and some of the dwellings scattered among the trees have a sameness of general shape that betrays their origin as camp buildings. BS&W closed their Myrtle Point site in 1926 and moved

Myrtle Point was once the site of one of BC's largest steam logging camps.

to even bigger things on Vancouver Island, but their early Powell River workings were one of the key pieces in building a forest empire that would bring them back to the area thirty-three years later—as co-owners of the Powell River pulp mill.

The experience of the people who settled south of town was much like that of people on the lower coast and coastal pioneers generally. They were lonely. They travelled half the day to visit a neighbour and a whole weekend to go to a dance. Without roads, boats became central players in the life, like the little steamboat nicknamed "Lopsided Lily," operated by "Steamboat Bob," which the logging companies used to hire to go down to the stump ranches and round up young ladies to entertain the boys at camp dances.

"We'd walk the nine miles down to the beach to go to the dance," remembered Lillian Palliser, whose unconventional English stepfather homesteaded inaccessible Horseshoe Valley above Stillwater. "Then we'd catch a boat to go over to Lang Bay…Stillwater had dances the odd time, and Myrtle Point. We had one fellow, a big Swede, Johnny Ulrich—and he played the music for all the dances…accordion, and boy, could he ever play! The drunker he got, the better he played."

Itinerant preachers and salesmen who came by boat, like the Rev. George Pringle on his *Sky Pilot* and radio expert Jim Spilsbury on the *Five BR*, were valued as much for their stories and good company as their services. The stories the old-timers from this area tell tend to be grounded in weather and natural forces. Lillian Palliser recalled the dry summers that brought huge forest fires:

> We were supposed to get out of the valley every year. Half the time we didn't do it, but this time the fire was right on us—you could see the flames of it. So Grampa went out and dug a great

Westview was one of several communities that grew up outside the limits of the company town, eventually becoming the larger centre.

big hole in the garden, and Mother took all her windows out of the house. She said if she had her windows, she could always build another house around them. We took all her windows and put them on top of all her stuff that she had: pots and pans and household stuff. It all went into this hole. Then dirt was put all over the top of it. Then Grampa walked right over it—broke half the windows.

If it wasn't fire it was snow or flooding rain, and if it wasn't that, it was big winds like the hurricane that broke up the Reverend Pringle's service at Lang Bay on January 29, 1921:

Big trees commenced to fall, crashing down on all sides of us. We had to shout into one another's ears to make ourselves heard. We were thankful to get to Smith's little frame house (where despite the storm, there was an overflow crowd). I announced a hymn. We were just getting the quavers out of our voices when the window tumbled in on my back. It took us fifteen minutes to get it nailed back and I was somewhere in "secondly" when a wild blast started the building paper lining the walls coming down, covering up my congregation...I didn't attempt to finish.

Named for the mill town's kindly patriarch, Dwight Hall was its community centre and is still a busy meeting place.

To survive in places like these you had to prize independence over almost every other trait. As you get nearer to Powell River proper, however, the story changes. The very way Powell Riverites view their universe puts the "town" at the centre and everything else at the margins. Anything up in the direction of Lund is referred to as "north of town." Saltery Bay, Stillwater, Lang Bay and Black Point are all referred to as "south of town." It harks back to the day when the mill and the company that ran it were supreme. From the first days of the mill in 1911, the life Powell River offered was a highly regulated one, suited more to the type of person who was willing to endure shift work for a steady paycheque, something antithetical to the free-spirited settlers to the north and south of town. On top of this, Powell River was in its early days a total company town, where everything from the water you drank to the food you ate to the roof over your head was granted at the pleasure of the boss. It even had a store, which was actually called "the Company Store." Grandfatherly old Dr. Dwight Brooks of the Brooks-Scanlon partnership was famous for the attention he paid to every detail of life in town and cast an atmosphere of benign but claustrophobic paternalism over all proceedings. The townsite school was called Brooks High School and a grand community centre was called Dwight Hall, after Dr. Brooks. Company managers were equally famous for handing out five-dollar bills to men whose wives had just given birth, and for blacklisting those who dared to question company policy.

It was very much to escape this absolute company rule that renegades began setting up pirate communities just outside the company pale, first around Cranberry Lake, then Wildwood—a favourite with Italian workers—and then the one that really took: Westview. By 1955 the company had acknowledged that its private kingdom had been superseded and sold off its residences. The *Powell River News* lamented, "Few better administered or generally happier company-controlled districts could be found in BC. Rents were low, there were no taxes for employees and all homes were maintained in first class repair. The 'Company Town Complex' was never evident in Powell River. Employees...look back with a degree of nostalgia to pre-1955 days."

Memories of what company town life was really like had to die down before nostalgia could blossom fully, but in recent years a vigorous restoration project has launched a campaign to restore and celebrate the old townsite, both the commercial section down by the mill and the residential section up on the hill above. It is one of those heritage sites whose importance is not so much in the quality of its architecture as in the history it represents. The guidebook *Sunshine and Salt Air* contains a good historical commentary on the townsite by local writer Karen Southern.

With the divestiture of the company-owned townsite, the separate villages of Cranberry Lake and Westview and the area of Wildwood were amalgamated with the old Powell River townsite to create the new Corporation of the District of Powell River. On the whole I have to agree with my dad about the results of this marriage. It did create a very vigorous, productive and at least outwardly contented community. Because the mill remained its central influence and focus, the combined community stayed unified after democratization, very much at odds with the anarchic style of the smaller logging and fishing villages of the Baja Sunshine Coast. Powell River people tend to mark off the periods of their lives not by timber claims they logged or fishboats they owned, but by the startup date of the first Kamyr digester or when the Number Seven Paper Machine shut down. Social relationships are influenced not

Cranberry Pottery, founded 1974, is the flagship of Powell River's vibrant craft scene.

Cranberry Lake was one of the renegade communities set up to avoid townsite rules but is now part of the District of Powell River. *Darren Robinson*

147

Above: Entertainers take the funky stage at the farmers' market at Paradise Valley Exhibition Park.

Right: The historic Patricia Theatre, a restored art deco movie house, is the showpiece of Powell River's restoration project.
Keith Thirkell

by neighbourhood so much as by mill shifts, as in "The Onderdonks lived just down the block but we never saw much of them because their men worked the 'A' shift and ours worked the 'B' shift."

The town never lacked for good community centres and it seethed with group activities. The largest ongoing feature in the community history *Pulp, Paper and People* by Karen Southern and Peggy Bird is one called "Clubs of the Decade," which follows the doings of groups like the Powell River Cricket Club, Powell River Pipe Band, Otago Rugby Club, and Women of the Moose. Community life centred on church activities, organized sports, social clubs and various artistic endeavours. As a bubble of ordered society surrounded by wilderness and isolated from any near neighbour, Powell River learned to be self-sufficient to the point of xenophobia. There was an "Us-Against-the-World" spirit that propelled participants to national and world class achievement in many areas.

In sports, Danny Lucas and Gary Lupul, products of the Powell River Minor Hockey Association, went on to play in the National Hockey League with the Philadelphia Flyers and the Vancouver Canucks. The Gerela brothers, Roy and Ted, made their name in pro football, Ted with the BC Lions and Roy with the Houston Oilers and Pittsburgh Steelers. Doug Ladret scored a top-ten finish in pairs figure skating competition at the 1988 Olympics.

Musicians Alicia Poot and Matthew Maffett, visiting for Kathaumixw, play their instruments on the Powell River waterfront.
Keith Thirkell

The town's strong interest in the arts attracted talented instructors who began turning out star pupils. Ballet teacher Frieda Shaw saw one ex-pupil, Onna White, claim an Oscar for her choreography of the movie *Oliver* in 1969, while another, Norman Thompson, went on to become state director for the Vienna Opera House. Don Thompson graduated from Paul Daugherty's music classes to become a Juno Award-winning jazz player. Silver Donald Cameron, whose educator father gave his name to the now-demolished Max Cameron High School, made his own name familiar across Canada as a bestselling journalist and author. In commerce, Peter Toigo learned business basics helping his mom and pop run their Wildwood grocery store from the time he could see over the meat counter, subdivided a farm while he was still in high school, and went on to become one of the province's high-profile tycoons as owner of the White Spot Restaurant chain, among other holdings.

It is typical of Powell River that the activity which has spread its name farthest is one of the most communal of all—choral singing. Again it was the presence of an exceptional leader in the person of choirmaster Don James that led to the creation of several highly successful choirs. They won many awards performing in Germany, Poland, Mexico, England and the Soviet Union. Building on this success, in 1984 Powell River began hosting a biannual choral festival called Kathaumixw (Ka-thou-mew), a triumphant event that attracts people from all over the world. In the realm of international choral singing, Powell River is a Bayreuth or Salzburg.

Leaving Powell River and heading north, the story is pretty much a replay of the one to the south, except for the Sliammon First Nation reserve just outside Wildwood. Sliammon offers

Right: Betty Wilson teaches
traditional Sliammon arts such as
basket weaving.

Below: A cedar-root basket in
Betty Wilson's collection.

Bottom: Sliammon Church.

no showpiece theatre-museum complex like its Sechelt counterpart, but the band is roughly equal in size and shares a similar history as a survivor of the Durieu system. Unlike Sechelt, the present Sliammon reserve is the Sliammon Band's traditional home, although it once shared winter quarters with the Klahoose and Homathco bands in Grace Harbour, a small bay in nearby Malaspina Inlet. Known as Kahkaykay, this winter meeting place must have been even more congested than Kalpalin.

Just north of Sliammon is an amorphous area known as Southview. The waterfront is peppered with residences and on the back land you can see scattered acreages dotted with skunk cabbage, marestail and the odd item of livestock that looks as if it would be happier wearing gumboots. The continental breadbasket it's not, though a few hardy stump ranchers supply a small but grateful following.

Donkeys watch over the Wildwood neighbourhood north of Powell River.

Top: The dock at Lund, now a pleasure boating base, was once the jumping-off point for work boats of the fishing and logging industries.

Above: Water taxis fan out from Lund to all parts of Desolation Sound and the northern gulf.

Left: The storied Lund Hotel was built by the founders of Lund in 1905.

Nancy's Bakery is a Lund institution.

TWENTY MILES NORTH OF POWELL RIVER is the village of Lund, a charming harbour community reminiscent of Egmont or Pender Harbour, with a small population of commercial fishboats and an interesting collection of character boats at the "guvermint worf." Lund's glory is the Malaspina Hotel, a handsome turn-of-the-century structure that is probably the single most historic building left on the rural BC coast, now that some halfwit developer has torched the Minstrel Island Hotel and Comox's The Lorne has fallen victim to fire. The Malaspina was built by Charles and Fredrick (Poppa) Thulin, two Swedish visionaries who founded the town of Lund in 1890, when their only company apart from the Texada towns would have been Leonard Frolander down at his Myrtle Point fur trading post, and possibly the unfortunate Jack Green, who officially opened his log cabin store on Savary Island in 1888.

Green is undisputed holder of the title of the first individual of European ancestry to be murdered on the Sunshine Coast, having been knocked on the head in 1893 by one Hugh Lynn, who subsequently became the first Sunshine Coast individual of any ancestry to be hanged by the neck. Green's game had been to offer provisions and small but very pricey snorts of firewater to the solitary handloggers who were working their way north by rowboat,

looking for "stumpers"—jumbo fir trees overhanging the water that, when they were chopped down, would jump from the stump straight into the saltchuck.

By Thulins' time, the stumpers were all stumped and loggers were having to bring larger crews into the upcoast jungles to extract timber by oxen, horses and railroads. Their operations begat a stream of powerboat traffic funnelling into Calm Channel. The Thulins' plan was to offer steam towboats a last chance to get groceries, cordwood and larger but still pricey snorts of firewater before heading north into the Yaculta rapids, and it proved good business. Within a few years they had two hotels, three stores, a large steamer dock and their own very handsome but preposterously named towboat the *Niluht* (figure it out.)

Lund is listed in more trivia books than any town of its size in Canada owing to its position as the end of the road—the longest road in the world. There is a sign near the wharf noting that this is the northern terminus of Highway 101, a.k.a. the Pan American Highway, which begins in Terra del Fuego and ends here peering over the guardrail at the Lund gas dock. A small but very dedicated movement convenes every night in the Malaspina Hotel bar (and all day on Saturdays) for the purpose of reversing the Pan American Highway so the end would be in Chile and Lund would have the beginning. I never miss a session without regretting it. There is no better place to lay over a bit and ponder the history that has streamed through the venerable Malaspina portals in the course of the century, the loafers and the muckers in pursuit of their contrary obsessions, modifying this sometimes sunshiney tract of real estate as they went, smudging its beauty here and there but finally posing only an indifferent challenge to its magnificence.

With its many inlets, lakes and islands, the Powell River area is prime paddling country.

155

Above: The new Mile 0 monument bolsters Lund's claim to being the start rather than the end of the Pan American Highway.

Above right: Spring morning in Lund.

In his pensive 1932 novella, *The Western Wall*, Hubert Evans pronounced what could be the final word on those restless seekers, loafers and muckers both. Now that their search for different ways has fetched them up against this wall of western ocean, he wrote, drawing them together in the realization that there is nowhere further to go, they must finally turn and face the task of forging a livable world together. Sometimes, as I eavesdrop on the fishermen at the next table squabbling over the allocation of the last few beleagured coho, I am not sure Hubert's caveat is coming any closer to realization. Then, when I listen to the snaggle-toothed old logger on the other side of me say he's got so used to the new look in the woods it seems completely natural to pick up his sandwich wrappings and pack them out of the bush in his lunchbucket, I think maybe we are.

The spirit of the pioneers that hovers over the Malaspina bar makes such reflections unavoidable, though in the pleasantest possible way. A session there also has the quite magical effect, that whenever the travellers decide it is done, early or late, and once again mount the steps up to that incredibly long, incredibly winding road, they will discover it has indeed reversed itself, and a new opportunity to explore the Sunshine Coast in its endless diversity waits to begin.

FURTHER READING ON THE SUNSHINE COAST

Alsgard, A.H., *Powell River's First 50 Years*, Powell River News, Powell River, 1960.

Bradley, R. Ken, *Historic Railways of the Powell River Area*, B.C. Railway Historical Association, Victoria, 1982.

Calhoun, Bruce, *Mac and the Princess: The Story of Princess Louisa Inlet*, Ricwalt Publishing, Seattle, 1976.

Cameron, Anne, *A Whole Brass Band*, Harbour Publishing, Madeira Park, 1994.

———— *Selkie*, Harbour Publishing, Madeira Park, 1996.

———— *The Whole Fam Damily*, Harbour Publishing, Madeira Park, 1995.

Carson, Bryan et al, *Sunshine and Salt Air: A Recreation Guide to the Sunshine Coast*, Harbour Publishing, Madeira Park, 1991 and 1997.

Dawe, Helen, *Helen Dawe's Sechelt*, Harbour Publishing, Madeira Park, 1990.

Evans, Hubert, *Mostly Coast People*, Harbour Publishing, Madeira Park, 1982.

Graham, Donald, *Lights of the Inside Passage: A History of BC's Lighthouses and Their Keepers*, Harbour Publishing, 1986.

Harbord, Heather, *Desolation Sound*, Harbour Publishing, Madeira Park, 2007.

———— *Texada Tapestry: A History*, Harbour Publishing, Madeira Park, 2011.

Hammond, Dick, *Tales From Hidden Basin*, Harbour Publishing, Madeira Park, 1996.

Hill-Tout, Charles, *The Salish People Vol. IV: The Sechelt and the South Eastern Tribes of Vancouver Island*, Talonbooks, Vancouver, 1978.

Iglauer, Edith, *Fishing With John*, Harbour Publishing, Madeira Park, 1988.

Keller, Betty C., and Leslie, Rosella, *Bright Seas, Pioneer Spirits: The Sunshine Coast*, Horsdal & Schubart, 1996.

Kennedy, Dorothy, and Bouchard, Randy, *Sliammon Life, Sliammon Lands*, Talonbooks, Vancouver, 1983.

Kennedy, Ian, *Sunny Sandy Savary: A History of Savary Island 1792–1992*, Kennell Publishing, Vancouver, 1992.

Lawrence, Grant, *Adventures in Solitude*, Harbour Publishing, 2010.

Mason, Elda Copley, *Lasqueti Island: History and Memory*, Byron Mason, Lantzville, 1975.

McIntyre, Margaret, *Place of Quiet Waters*, Longmans Canada, Don Mills, 1965.

Peterson, Lester, *The Gibsons Landing Story*, Peter Martin Books Canada, 1962.

———— *The Story of the Sechelt Nation*, Harbour Publishing, Madeira Park, 1990.

Roberts Creek Historical Society, *Remembering Roberts Creek 1889–1955*, Harbour Publishing, Madeira Park, 1978.

Roberts, Harry, *The Trail of Chack Chack*, Carlton, New York, 1968.

Rubin, Dan, *Salt on the Wind: The Sailing Life of Allen and Sharie Farrell*, Horsdal and Schubart, 1996.

Schweizer, W.H. *Beyond Understanding: The Complete Guide to Princess Louisa Inlet, Chatterbox Falls, Jervis Inlet*, EOS Publishing, Seattle, 1989.

Sinclair, B.W. *Poor Man's Rock*, Little Brown, New York, 1920.

Smart, Elizabeth, *By Grand Central Station I Sat Down and Wept*, Deneau Publishers, Ottawa, 1981.

Southern, Karen, and Bird, Peggy, *Pulp, Paper and People: 75 Years of Powell River*, Powell River Heritage Research Association, Powell River, 1990.

———— *The Nelson Island Story*, Hancock House, Surrey, 1987.

Spilsbury, Jim, *Spilsbury's Album*, Harbour Publishing, Madeira Park, 1987.

Thompson, Bill, *Boats, Bucksaws and Blisters: Pioneer Tales of the Powell River Area*, Powell River Heritage Research Association, Powell River, 1993.

———— *Once Upon A Stump: Times and Tales of Powell River Pioneers*, Powell River Heritage Research Association, Powell River, 1993.

Trower, Peter, *Grogan's Cafe*, Harbour Publishing, Madeira Park, 1995.

———— *Haunted Hills and Hanging Valleys, Selected Poems 1969–2004*, Harbour Publishing, 2004.

White, Howard, and Spilsbury, Jim, *Spilsbury's Coast*, Harbour Publishing, Madeira Park, 1987.

———— *The Accidental Airline*, Harbour Publishing, Madeira Park, 1988.

White, Howard, ed. *Raincoast Chronicles First Five*, Harbour Publishing, Madeira Park, 1976.

———— *Raincoast Chronicles Six-Ten*, Harbour Publishing, Madeira Park, 1983.

———— *Raincoast Chronicles Eleven Up*, Harbour Publishing, Madeira Park, 1994.

White, Howard, *Ghost in the Gears*, Harbour Publishing, Madeira Park, 1993.

———— *Writing in the Rain*, Harbour Publishing, Madeira Park, 1990.

White, Stewart Edward, *Skookum Chuck*, Garden City, New York, 1925.

INDEX

Acknowledgements

This book would not have been possible but for the remarkable pool of photographic talent that exists on the Sunshine Coast. Dean van't Schip led the way and Keith Thirkell and Allan Forest (www.allanforest.com) made major contributions. Others including Darren Robinson and the Sunshine Coast Museum and Archives added essential pieces. The aerial photographs taken by Dean van't Schip appear courtesy Richard Rudnisky, who generously provided flying time. Boat travel in Hotham Sound was kindly provided by Mike Nicholson and in Princess Louisa Inlet by Sunshine Coast Tours. I am indebted to Candy Clarke, Theresa Jeffries, Ann Quinn, Karen Southern and Brin Wilson for their expert suggestions on the manuscript. This book is dedicated to my dad, Frank White, a builder of the Sunshine Coast.

Text copyright © 1996, 2011 Howard White
Photographs copyright © Dean van't Schip except where noted

1 2 3 4 5 — 15 14 13 12 11

Harbour Publishing Co. Ltd.
P.O. Box 219, Madeira Park, BC, V0N 2H0
www.harbourpublishing.com

Front end sheet map courtesy the Sunshine Coast Museum and Archives
Back end sheet map by Roger Handling
Text design by Roger Handling, Terra Firma Digital Arts
Printed and bound in Canada

 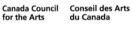

Harbour Publishing acknowledges financial support from the Government of Canada through the Canada Book Fund and the Canada Council for the Arts, and from the Province of British Columbia through the BC Arts Council and the Book Publishing Tax Credit.

Library and Archives Canada Cataloguing in Publication

White, Howard, 1945–   The Sunshine Coast : from Gibsons to Powell River / Howard White ; photography by Dean van't Schip ... [et al.]. — 2nd ed.

Includes index.
ISBN 978-1-55017-552-3

1. Sunshine Coast (B.C.)—History. 2. Sunshine Coast (B.C.)—Description and travel. 3. Sunshine Coast (B.C.)—Pictorial works. I. Van't Schip, Dean, 1962- II. Title.

FC3845.S95W55 2011   971.1'31   C2011-904632-6

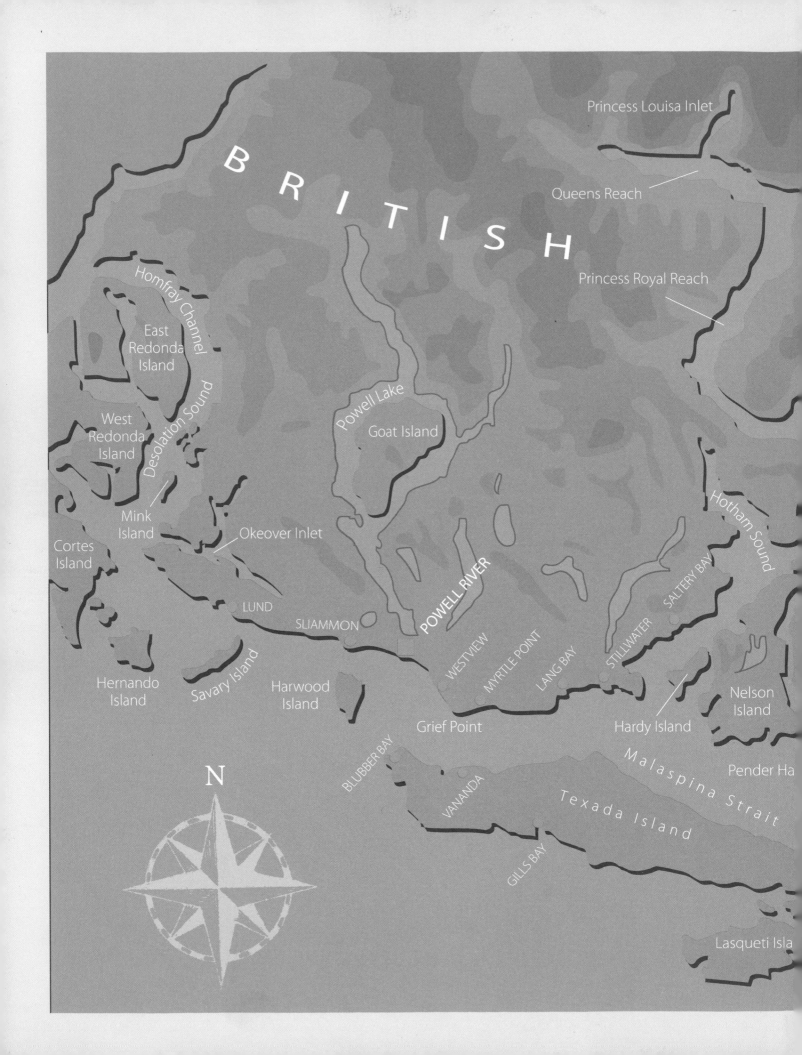